HOW
GOD
ANSWERS
PRAYER

BOOKS BY ELMER L. TOWNS

How God Answers Prayer

Knowing God Through Fasting

*Praying for Your Second Chance: Prayers
from Numbers and Deuteronomy*

Praying Genesis

Praying Paul's Letters

Praying the Book of Acts and the General Epistles

Praying the Book of Job

Praying the Book of Revelation

Praying the Gospels

Praying the New Testament

Praying the Proverbs, Song of Solomon, and Ecclesiastes

Praying the Psalms

Praying With the Conquerors: Praying Joshua, Judges, and Ruth

Praying Your Way Out of Bondage: Prayers from Exodus and Leviticus

AVAILABLE FROM DESTINY IMAGE PUBLISHERS

How
GOD
Answers
Prayer

Elmer L. Towns

DESTINY IMAGE® PUBLISHERS, INC.

P.O. Box 310, Shippensburg, PA 17257-0310

"Speaking to the Purposes of God for This Generation and for the Generations to Come."

This book and all other Destiny Image, Revival Press, MercyPlace, Fresh Bread, Destiny Image Fiction, and Treasure House books are available at Christian bookstores and distributors worldwide.

For a U.S. bookstore nearest you, call 1-800-722-6774.
For more information on foreign distributors, call 717-532-3040.
Reach us on the Internet: www.destinyimage.com.

ISBN 10: 0-7684-3114-X
ISBN 13: 978-0-7684-3114-8

For Worldwide Distribution, Printed in the U.S.A.
1 2 3 4 5 6 7 8 9 10 11 / 13 12 11 10 09

CONTENT

SECTION III
The Way God Gives Answers

SECTION IV
The "No" Answers to Our Prayers

PREFACE

Looking for Answers

The purpose of this book is not to tell you how to get answers to your prayers. There are thousands of books like that. This book approaches prayer from the other end—God's end. This is a radically different book because it describes what God does to answer prayers.

Remember, prayer is *relationship with God*, so when we ask Him for something, the issue is "How does God respond?"

Let's play a game! Pretend you are a small kid who begs for something from your mother. Then compare this illustration to praying Christians who ask God for something. Many times our mothers respond like God when He hears our request.

When I was a kid on a rainy afternoon, I'd ask Mom, "What ya got to eat?" If this were a typical book on prayer, we would examine how to make the request to Mother, or God, when to ask, and attitudes that prompt the anticipated response.

Since this book looks at *How God Answers Prayer*, let's examine the various ways my mom answered me. Mom often got me involved, saying, "Let's get some cocoa and make fudge," or she would send me searching, "You'll find some cookies in the jar," or she put me to work, "Get some money off the mantelpiece and go buy a cake mix from the store."

Just as there are lots of ways that a mother answers her child's request, there are lots of ways God answers our prayers. God doesn't always give us an answer sometimes He tells us to get involved in the answer, or go look for the answer, or to work for the answer.

Notice some other answers: "No…it's too close to dinner," or "No, you've had too much sugar today," or "No…you just had something to eat a few minutes ago." God may also answer our prayers, "No, the answer would hurt you," or "No, I don't do it that way," or "No…I recently answered the opposite way."

There are other ways mothers answer a child's request: "You don't need candy, let's have some soup," or "How about some leftover fried chicken?" or "You didn't eat all your veggies at lunch." Now then, God uses the same answers: "That answer is not good for you, I'll give you a healthy answer," or "Why don't you search the Scripture for your answer?"

Most books on prayer tell you that God may say "No" when you ask. But this book tells you several different ways God says "No."

Again, most books on prayer tell you that God may say "Wait" as one of His answers. But this book tells you that there are several reasons why God wants you to wait.

And when it comes to answering prayers, this book tells you several different ways God answers your prayers.

So as you read, you will learn some things that you've never considered. When you learn about prayer from God's perspective, maybe you will pray more intelligently to get the answer you seek. Maybe you won't tell God how to answer your prayer, but you'll trust Him to answer your prayers in His own way. And maybe this book will take away some of your discouragement when you understand why God says "No."

So, if you don't get your prayer answered when you want it, how you want it, and the way you want it, go back to our premise—*prayer is relationship*. Don't be like the little child who goes into his room to pout because Mother won't give him all the fudge he wants. It could be the mother knows that each time her child has fudge, he gets a stomachache. Maybe Mother has something better for the child than fudge. Maybe she has strawberry shortcake—with fresh strawberries—and real whipped cream waiting for him instead. Maybe Mother knows you like strawberry shortcake better than fudge. But if you go to your room and whine, you may not get fudge *or* strawberry shortcake.

When you understand *How God Answers Prayer*, then you realize prayer is all about trusting your heavenly Father. You must trust Him to answer *what* is best for you…*how* it's best for you…and *when* it's best for you. Remember, God loves you and has a wonderful plan for your life. You can find that plan through praying properly, and you may get some strawberry shortcake with real strawberries and whipped cream.

Sincerely yours in Christ,
Elmer L. Towns
Written from my home
at the foot of the Blue Ridge Mountains

SECTION

THE WAY GOD PROMISED
HE WOULD ANSWER

Just as a little girl knows *when* to ask her father for something she wants, she also knows *how* to ask, and *how much* to ask. So we must remember prayer is relationship with God. We must know how to relate to Him to get our answers.

Yes we must ask, but ask because we obey His commandments. Then we ask because we have spiritual fruit in our lives and because we have faith in God. Also, we must not be rebellious against Him, nor sin, nor must we ask for things contrary to Scriptures.

Asking is the rule of the Kingdom and we must learn how to follow God's rules to get God's answers.

Asking Answers

The Blind Bartimaeus Factor—God Answers by Giving Us the Things for Which We Ask

BARTIMAEUS WAS A BEGGAR WHO sat at the gate to Jericho begging for alms. Jesus came by with His disciples, and Bartimaeus asked what all the commotion was about. He was told, *"Jesus of Nazareth is passing by"* (Luke 18:37).

In response, Bartimaeus began to yell out loud, *"Jesus, Son of David, have mercy on me"* (Luke 18:38).

Those around him tried to keep him quiet, but he cried out all the more, *"Son of David, have mercy on me!"* (Luke 18:39).

Jesus heard Bartimaeus crying out, so He went to the blind man. Jesus asked, *"What do you want me to do for you?"*

All Bartimaeus knew was the voice of Jesus who was speaking to him. He said, *"Lord, that I may receive my sight"* (Luke 18:41). In calling Jesus "Lord," Bartimaeus probably included all the worship of deity that was in his heart.

Bartimaeus had a very simple request, although extraordinary in scope. A man who was blind was asking for his sight. Jesus responded, *"Receive your sight; your faith has made you well"* (Luke 18:42). Then Bartimaeus could see, just because he asked for sight.

One of the key ingredients of prayer is asking.

When I was a 17-year-old freshman at Columbia Bible College, I was in a dormitory with World War II veterans who had been influenced during the war by a group called the Navigators. Most of these men had small notebooks where they kept their Bible study material, but they also had pages where they wrote out their requests for prayer. Each page contained a list of the simple things for which these men were praying. I purchased a small notebook and also began a prayer list. I still have most of those pages of prayer lists that go back to the 1950s.

During that time I tried to date three or four freshman girls who were cute and had a lot of sparkle. But when I asked them for dates, I was turned down because one girl had to "wash her hair," another had to "study," the third to "write a term paper." I didn't quite believe them; I just thought they didn't want to go out with me.

In January 1951, I picked out Ruth Forbes, one of the best-looking girls at the college, the most spiritual, whose father had lots of money. I wrote in my prayer list, RUTH FORBES, and began banging on the windows of Heaven to get the attention of God by saying, "God, when I ask Ruth to go out with me on a date, make her say 'YES!'"

When I finally asked her out, she said, "Sure, why not?"

We went on a date more for friendship than any other reason. Then I found myself dating her for how fun it was to be with her; not for romantic love or even puppy love. We just had so much in common; we prayed together, served the Lord together, and later when I became pastor of a weekend church in Savannah, Georgia, we used our Friday night dates to write, type, and print the church bulletins on a mimeograph machine in the student lounge.

I learned that you should ask for the things you want, even dates in college. Why? Because *the Lord loves to answer your prayers.*

In September 1951, after ten months of dating, Ruth and I began to get serious about each other. Her name was no longer in the middle of my prayer list, but was number one at the top of the page.

Again I banged on the windows of Heaven, asking God, "When I ask her to marry me, make her say 'Yes!'"

Finally, toward the end of September, I picked a rose from a neighbor's yard next to the college, had my proposal poem written, and knelt before her. I asked her if she would be my wife. God answered my prayer. She said, "Sure, why not?" (She didn't really say that. She was as scared as I was at the moment, and she said, "Mmmm, huh!")

To this day I tell young people at Liberty University, don't even think about marrying someone you can't pray with. As a matter of fact, don't even go out with that person if you can't pray together on your date.

When we think that prayer is simply asking, remember the words of James, *"You do not have because you do not ask"* (James 4:2).

After Ruth and I had been married about 25 years, I found myself walking through a city park in Savannah, Georgia, my home. I saw a middle-aged woman sitting on a park bench who nodded to me, and I nodded back but kept walking. She said, "Elmer Towns." She recognized me, so I said,

"Yes."

She said, "I'm Betty (and she gave her last name)."

I remembered Betty from our high school days; she was a petite beauty who could have been a high school cheerleader; her personality and good looks could have opened any door she wanted. Betty had been saved in the same revival meeting where I came to know Christ as my Savior. We passed a few pleasantries; then she asked,

"How come you never asked me for a date when we were in high school…?"

I backed away, a little embarrassed and a little afraid. I had heard that Betty had a "spoiled reputation," gone through a couple of marriages, and was no longer living for God. I didn't know what she was suggesting, but I didn't want any part of it.

Betty said, "Of all the boys in high school, I always wanted to date you, but you never asked me."

I remembered that she dated Charles the big football guy, and Arthur the big basketball guy; she had always gone for the sports guys. Then she explained,

"I always wanted to date you, because you worked so hard; you had a paper route in the morning and a paper route at night, and you made a lot of money. I knew you would take care of me."

At that moment I realized I could have dated her, but I was too reluctant to ask her. I thought I was not good enough. At that moment, the Scripture popped into my head, *"You have not because you ask not"* (see James 4:2).

Isn't that true of many of us? We don't ask God for the great things that we want him to do because we think we are not good enough (see Chapter 4) or we are too aware of our sin. Remember the blind Bartimaeus principle: God answers by giving us the things for which we ask.

Let's Pray Now

Since God expects you to ask, and God answers when you ask, the next step is to learn how to ask God to answer your prayers. Let the following principles guide you.

First, pray specifically… *"If you ask anything in My name, I will do it"* (John 14:14).

Second, pray according to the Word of God… *"If you abide in Me, and My words abide in you, you will ask what you desire, and it shall be done for you"* (John 15:7).

Third, pray as you try to win lost people to Christ. *"…That you should go and bear fruit…that whatever you ask the Father in My name He may give you"* (John 15:16).

Fourth, live a life of obedience that backs up your prayer… *"Whatever we ask we receive from Him, because we keep His commandments…"* (1 John 3:22).

Fifth, don't quit praying… *"Continue asking, and it will be given to you"* (Matt. 7:7 PEB).

Sixth, ask in faith… *"whatever things you ask when you pray, believe that you receive them, and you will have them"* (Mark 11:24).

God loves it when you ask Him for things—asking is a rule in God's family. So begin your prayer list like I began mine in 1950. Begin banging on the door of Heaven for answers. God loves to answer prayers.

2

Faith Answers

The Syrophoenician Woman Factor: God Answers in Response to When We Believe in Him

ASYROPHOENICIAN WOMAN CAME BEGGING to Jesus, *"Have mercy on me, O Lord, Son of David! My daughter is severely demon possessed"* (Matt. 15:22).

Jesus didn't answer the woman, and the disciples wanted to send her away. At that time, Jesus explained why He didn't answer the woman, *"I was not sent except to the lost sheep of the house of Israel"* (Matt. 15:24). Jesus was giving a theological answer, *"to the Jew first and also for the Greek"* (Rom. 1:16). But the woman didn't care about theology; she kept praying, *"Lord, help me"* (Matt. 15:25).

The Lord heard her plea, but He again answered her saying, *"It is not good to take the children's bread and throw it to the little dogs"* (Matt. 15:26). Here, Jesus was referring to the habit of feeding dogs that were under the family table during meal time. The term "dogs" was a Jewish term used to refer to Gentiles.

But the woman explained, *"Yes, Lord, yet even the little puppies eat the crumbs which fall from their master's table."* Jesus commented, *"O woman, great is your faith. Be it to you as you desire"* (Matt 15:27-28).

What impressed Jesus about this woman? First of all He saw her deep faith in Him to answer her request. Second, He felt the pressure of her persistent request. What she wanted in faith is what Jesus gave to her.

What is praying in faith? It is knowing that God can give you what you request, and that you'll know God will answer long before the answer comes.

In the winter of 1979, Jerry Falwell walked into chapel of Liberty University and announced that he was canceling the program for that day. "We're all going to walk up to those seven buildings on the hill that are half finished. We're going to ask God to send in five million dollars to complete construction."

Falwell went on to explain that any student who was "with him" could follow him up to the construction site. "Walk around the buildings one time when you get there," he explained. "We don't have time to walk around seven times." Then he said, "Kneel in groups of seven, and each pray asking God for five million dollars."

As Falwell jumped from the platform to head for the door, I followed him. We marched up the street and around the buildings one time. Then I knelt in a group with seven Liberty administrators, and I was the first to pray,

"Lord, five million dollars is more money than I've ever seen or touched. I don't have faith to ask you for five million dollars. That's more money than I can even dream of. Lord, I can't ask You for money, I ask You to give me faith to believe You for great things."

I didn't realize that television cameras were capturing what we prayed, and the following week I heard myself announce to the nation on television, "I don't have faith…Lord; I believe, help my unbelief."

Then the television screened zeroed in on Jerry Falwell who prayed, "Lord, You've got a lot of money and I need some of it. I need five million dollars to finish these seven buildings, and I need it right away. When I get five million dollars, we can train eight hundred more young people who will be pastors, missionaries, lawyers, and teachers. Lord, I know You will send this money, so I will tell the contractor to get started tomorrow morning. Within a couple of weeks I will need to make my first payment, so I trust You for the money to come in right away."

I'd listened to the confidence of Falwell's prayer and it blew me away. He really believed that the money was coming. I interviewed him for a story and began to dig deep, "Did you really believe the money was coming in?"

"Yes."

I went to his wife, Macel, and asked the same question, "Did Jerry really believe the money was coming in?"

"Yes."

To the amazement of all, the money came in and the dorms were finished, and an additional 800 students were added to Liberty University that year. God honored the prayer of faith.

Jerry answered me, "Didn't Jesus say that if we prayed in faith He would give us what we ask?" He quoted, *"Therefore I say to you, whatever things you ask when you pray, believe that you receive them, and you will have them"* (Mark 11:24).

One of the foremost conditions for getting answers to prayer is to pray in faith. *"But without faith it is impossible to please Him, for he who comes to God must believe that He is, and that He is a rewarder of those who diligently seek Him"* (Heb. 11:6). Therefore, from this one verse we see two conditions of prayer. First, we must have absolute faith that God exists and hears us. Second, we must "diligently seek Him." Therefore, the Syrophenecian Woman Factor must be followed: God answers in response to our persistent faith.

LET'S PRAY NOW

Great faith is not measured by your sincerity, your ability to believe, or anything within your heart. A man with strong muscles, and a man with weak muscles—barely able to move—can both switch on an electric light. It's not the power of the man who throws the switch that determines if the lights will come on. No, not at all. It's the power of the generator that supplies the energy for the lights.

Once I complimented Jerry Falwell for his great faith, but he corrected me. "I don't have great faith, I have faith in a great God." The size of your God determines the answer to your prayers, not the size of your faith.

Jesus said, "…*if you have faith as a mustard seed…*" (Matt. 17:20). A mustard seed was so small that Jesus was saying, "If you have a little faith, as opposed to no faith—you could move mountains or God."

So how can you get more faith to become the one who can move God? Get a bigger God. First, learn about Him from Scripture. Second, read the stories of great heroes of the faith; get their vision of God. Third, rely on your God for answers, not on your ability to pray.

Remember, "…*all things are possible to him who believes*" (Mark 9:23).

3

Fasting Answers

The Hannah Factor—God Answers
When We Fast and Pray

Hannah was one of the first people in the Bible to get an answer to prayer because she prayed deeply and fasted to God for an answer to a distressing need. She was married to a man named Elkanah who had two wives. The Bible describes this situation, but does not condone it to us. (The Bible teaches one man for one woman for one lifetime.)

Elkanah's first wife had children. The Bible says Elkanah's first wife *"provoked her* [Hannah] *severely to make her miserable"* (1 Sam. 1:6). Apparently there was tremendous rivalry between the two wives married to Elkanah.

The childless wife, Hannah, *"prayed to the Lord and wept in anguish"* (1 Sam. 1:10). She even added a vow to her prayer that if God would give her a son, she would dedicate that boy to the Lord all the days of his life (1 Sam. 1:11).

Added to Hannah's intercession was fasting. Her husband said, *"Why do you not eat?"* (1 Sam. 1:8). Eli the high priest saw her in the tabernacle praying and thought she was drunk because she prayed so earnestly, and probably outwardly emotionally. Eli assured her that her prayers would be answered, *"So, the woman* [Hannah] *went her way and ate…"* (1 Sam. 1:18). She terminated her fast, *"…and the Lord remembered her.… Hannah conceived and bore a son and called his name Samuel, saying, 'because I have asked him from the Lord'"* (1 Sam. 1:19-20).

The Bible gives many illustrations of people getting their prayers answered because they fasted and prayed, including Ezra, Nehemiah, Elijah, John the Baptist, and Paul (see my book *Fasting for Spiritual Breakthrough*).

I had never fasted technically before I came to help start Liberty University, although there were times I went without eating to study in preparation for a sermon, or in traveling to preach a sermon. When I got busy in God's work, I just didn't eat. I'd never engaged in what Jesus calls *"prayer and fasting"* (Matt. 17:21).

As I was helping Jerry Falwell start Liberty University, approximately four months into the school year Jerry announced that we would fast and pray for a million dollars for the new college. That was threatening because as a leader of the University, I felt I ought to be the example. I thought fearfully, *What if I fast and faint in front of my students?* or, *What if I get sick and throw up in front of my students?*

Obviously I was more afraid of what people thought of me than what I thought about God and what He could do through that fast.

I kept praying, "God, help me get through this fast." It was a constant prayer. After my first one-day fast, the only thing God did for me—He answered that prayer; I got through my fast, but that was all.

A few months later, I decided to put fasting to the test. My wife and I owned a home in greater Chicago and we were also making house payments on a home in Lynchburg, Virginia. So I said to Ruth, "Let's fast and ask God to sell the house in greater Chicago."

We fasted on the fifteenth day of that month because our Chicago house payment was due on the fifteenth. Nothing happened. I forgot about it until the following month when writing my check for the Chicago house, so I said, "Let's fast again on the fifteenth day to sell the house."

We continued to fast on each fifteenth day of the month, and I have to admit, without a great amount of faith. Chicago was in the grips of a down market for real estate. Finally after a year, the house sold and I went to Chicago for the closing. The purchaser casually mentioned, "My wife and I first visited your house on her birthday." I didn't really pay attention to him until he mentioned it was the sixteenth day of the month, the day after we first fasted.

The hair on the back of my head bristled, and I shuddered all over in fear. They visited the house the day after we fasted the first time. Then the purchaser told me he came back about once a month and couldn't get our house out of his mind. At that moment I realized three things happen when you pray and fast.

First, fasting takes your prayer to a higher level so that you will get an answer. Second, fasting is effective when you fast and pray with another person (see Matt. 18:19). And third, once you begin praying, don't give up. I had the distinct impression that if we had not continued fasting in prayer, the purchaser would not have come back and looked at our house again and again.

LET'S PRAY NOW[1]

You should begin your first fast the way I still fast for one day. It's called a *Yom Kippur Fast*, which is what the conscientious Jew still does today. On the appointed day, you *"must spend the day in self-examination.... It is a Sabbath of solemn rest for you, and you shall spend the day in quiet humility (fasting)"* (Lev. 16:29,31 ELT).

The Jews measure a day just as God did when creating the universe, *"So the evening and the morning were the first day"* (Gen. 1:5,8,13, 19,23,31). Since God begins a day with sundown, I begin a fast by missing the evening meal to spend that time in prayer. Then I go without eating breakfast and lunch, devoting much time to prayer.

Missing meals will not move the heart of God; it's relationship with Him that gets your prayers answered. So I spend my usual time of prayer on a fast-day, plus pray during the times of the meal itself.

Before beginning a fast, I write down the length of my fast (one day, three days, ten days, etc.) and I write down the specific purpose of a fast. Usually I don't fast for more than one specific reason, but during that fast-day, I obviously pray for all the requests on my prayer list.

On a one-day fast, I drink only water and coffee (plus take my vitamins); this is called a *normal fast*, or a *juice fast* (I drink juice for a fast longer than one day). An *absolute fast* is when I don't drink anything (but don't go for more than three days without drinking or you'll harm yourself physically.)

I wait for the sun to go down, then eat a normal meal. When I was in Israel, I asked my Jewish guide if he fasted on the Day of Atonement.

"Yes, of course," he answered.

Then I asked when he broke his fast. "The rabbis teach us we can't eat till we see two stars in the sky."

"Why is that?" I asked.

"A hungry man can see a single star that's not there," he answered.

If you want answers to your prayers, try fasting. It takes intercession to a higher level. It demonstrates your sincerity to God and tells Him, "This request is imperative!"

Endnote

1. See *Fasting for Spiritual Breakthrough* by Elmer Towns; Regal Books, Ventura, CA, 1996. This book is considered the most complete book on fasting because it suggests nine different fasts for nine different purposes, each one carried out in a different way.
   Visit www.regalbooks.com to order.

4

Jesus' Name Answers

The Peter Factor—God Answers
When We Pray in Jesus' Name

A 40-YEAR-OLD LAME MAN WHO had never walked begged for alms at the temple gate in Jerusalem (see Acts 3:2, 4:10). Apparently Peter and John went there every afternoon at approximately 3:00 P.M. to pray in the temple. As they entered, the man begged alms from Peter, who answered; *"In the name of Jesus Christ of Nazareth, rise up and walk"* (Acts 3:6).

Peter's faith is not mentioned as the reason God healed the man, nor was it the lame man's persistent prayer, nor anything that the human Peter did. When Peter prayed in Jesus' name, *"He* [the lame man] *leaping up stood...walking, leaping, and praising God"* (Acts 3:8).

Then the next day, Peter wanted to make sure everyone knew the source of the healing. He told the accusing Jews, *"...by the name of Jesus Christ of Nazareth, whom you crucified, whom God hath raised from the dead, by Him this man stands here before you whole"* (Acts 4:10).

Peter was applying the prayer principle that Jesus told him the night before He died. In the upper room Jesus said, *"Until now you have asked nothing in my name"* (John 16:24). This means they had been praying to Jehovah according to Old Testament principles, but from that moment on they would pray to the Father through Jesus. *"Ask and ye shall receive, that your joy may be full"* (John 16:24).

What does it mean to pray in Jesus' name?

First, we pray through Jesus the Intercessor who stands at the right hand of God the Father, making intercession for us (see Heb. 7:24-25). As our Intercessor, Jesus takes our requests and makes a perfect presentation to the Father.

Second, we pray through Jesus' accomplishments on the Cross. Since His blood cleanses us from all sin (see 1 John 1:7), then because of Jesus' cleansing of our sin, there is nothing that will block our intercession.

Third, we pray in Jesus' name because He indwells us: *"Christ lives in me"* (Gal. 2:20). The inner presence of Christ gives us direction and power in our prayer. Because Jesus indwells us, we can make effective intercession to the Father.

I love to hear Jack Hayford when he prays for lost people. He's the former pastor of the Church on the Way, Van Nuys, California. I have heard Jack say, "Lord, I agree with Jesus' prayer, *'For those who will believe in Me through their* (preached) *word'"* (John 17:20). When I hear Jack pray, I feel as if I'm standing in the throne room of Heaven, as he and Jesus are making intercession to the Father. Therefore, I enter that same throne room and pray, "Lord, I agree with Jesus, that *'the prayer of faith will save the sick'"* (James 5:15).

LET'S PRAY NOW

When you ask God for anything in prayer, it has a lot to do with *trust*. If you had two sisters and you were planning an anniversary meal for Mom, which sister would you ask? The first sister is detail-oriented and finishes everything she starts. The second sister is a little scatter brained and seems to never finish anything she starts. That's a no brainer; you'd ask the sister that you trust the most to do the best job. So when you ask God for anything, you demonstrate your trust in Him.

And isn't *asking* one of the most elementary forms of dependence? When children have to ask for a sandwich, or for anything from a parent, it reflects the child's trust in the person they ask. The child thinks the parent can supply it, and that by asking, the parent will give it.

Remember, God likes to be asked. Anyone who is a mother or father enjoys it when their children ask for things. Whether they're asking for a drink on a hot day, or for money to buy a hamburger, or for something big like their first bicycle or even their first car; love grows in an atmosphere of asking and giving.

There's another thing: when you ask God for anything, it puts you into partnership with your heavenly Father. Suppose you were put on a church committee where you had to work with another person. You'd have to ask and then receive advice from that other person. When you learn to ask things from God, you build a relationship and you are a co-worker with Him in the business of the Kingdom.

Finally, asking enriches your fellowship with God. When you open up your heart to God in prayer to ask for things that you need, it deepens your relationship with your heavenly Father.

But some people say, "I don't want to disturb God with minor things." Doesn't that suggest a breach in your fellowship with God? Would we worry about asking a close friend for something, or for anything, especially if we considered it a minor thing? On the other hand, even if you thought you could, you can't hide anything from God. He already knows what you need before you ask, so you might as well ask Him (see Matt. 6:8).

Suppose you didn't ask God for anything, at any time, for any reason. Suppose you kept all your prayers in that lofty area of worship, praise, and adoration. What if you never asked God for His help when you had a problem, or what if you never felt you could ask Him for things that you need? Would that be an honest relationship? No. So if you can't honestly ask God for things, can you honestly worship Him?

I love to say, "Asking is the rule of the kingdom." It's the way God does Kingdom business. Asking is not a lower form of prayer; but rather, asking is at the highest level where God is located. Since God is able to answer and God has promised to answer, God will answer—why don't you ask now?

5

Obedient Answers

*The Jonah Factor: We Must Obey to Get
the Thing for Which We Ask*

GOD RAISED UP PROPHETS IN the Old Testament to whom He spoke, then these men did the will of God. God came to Jonah with a special message, *"Now the word of the Lord came to Jonah…'Arise, go to Nineveh, that great city, and cry out against it; for their wickedness has come up before Me'"* (Jon. 1:1-2).

This was a very clear command from God; but Jonah not only chose to ignore what God said, he did the exact opposite, *"But Jonah arose to flee to Tarshish…"* (Jon. 1:3). Disobedience to God is sin. David the Psalmist tells us, *"If I regard iniquity in my heart, the Lord will not hear"* (Ps. 66:18). Again, we read in Scripture, *"Now we know that God does not hear sinners"* (John 9:31).

It just wasn't enough that Jonah disobeyed God; notice he forsook God's presence. *"But Jonah arose to flee to Tarshish from the presence of the Lord"* (Jon. 1:3). In one sense you can't run from God, for He is everywhere present. But this is *perceptual presence*; Jonah was running away from where he thought God was located. Since God called the Promised Land His land, and God lived in Jerusalem, Jonah wanted to get as far away from God and the Promised Land as possible.

The story is well known: *"But the Lord sent out a great wind…and there was a mighty tempest on the sea…"* (Jon. 1:4). You can't run from God—He will pursue you; and if necessary, punish you to bring you back to His will.

The captain and sailors onboard the ship realized God was punishing Jonah, so they threw him overboard and he was swallowed by a great fish.

Now we need to ask, "What happened spiritually to Jonah when he was punished by God?" *"Then Jonah prayed to the Lord his God from the fish's belly"* (Jon. 2:1).

Jonah began to repent when he said, *"I have been cast out of Your sight; yet I will look again toward Your holy temple"* (Jon. 2:4). He realized that the greatest sin was leaving the presence of God, not just disobeying the word of God. He confessed, *"When I had lost all hope, I turned my thoughts once more to the Lord"* (Jonah 2:7 TLB). And what does he do when he turns to God? *"My earnest prayer went to you"* (Jonah 2:7 TLB).

But Jonah took another step; he knew he had to confess his sins and offer a blood sacrifice in the Temple: *"I will never worship anyone but you! For how can I thank you enough for all you have done? I will surely fulfill my promises. For my deliverance comes from the Lord alone"* (Jonah 2:9 TLB).

Perhaps you are like Jonah and you have sin in your life. God will not hear your prayers until you repent in your heart which is turning to God. Then repent with your feet, meaning you are willing to turn around and go the opposite way. Third, you repent with your power of choice, meaning you are now willing to do God's will.

Once I asked Mother for a second piece of cake that she had just made. But she said, "No, you didn't do what I asked." Mother had asked me to bring in some kindling wood before supper. (I'm so old I remember when Mother baked cakes in a stove that used wood for heat.) I knew how much kindling wood was needed for the fire, so I skimped and just brought in enough to heat the oven and bake the cake. So I ate my first piece of cake and wanted more.

"No," mother said, "I had asked you to bring in kindling wood before dinner."

I had done two things wrong. First, I had not completely obeyed my mother to bring in enough kindling wood to cook dinner. There was another problem; I hadn't pleased Mother because I was a disobedient son.

Notice the same two things are necessary to get our prayers answered by God, "*...we keep His commandments and do those things that are pleasing in His sight*" (1 John 3:22).

This positive commandment carries the opposite negative warning, "No." We can't get our prayers answered if we break His commandments. Didn't the writer of Hebrews say, "*...he who comes to God must believe that He is, and that He is a rewarder of those who diligently seek Him*" (Heb. 11:6)?

One of my students told me he was switching from the pastoral major to become a school teacher.

"Why?" I asked.

"Because I found that God didn't answer my prayers."

When I interrogated him carefully, he said that he had prayed specifically for money to pay his bills and it did not come in. Then he went on to say that he had prayed for a specific girl, one he thought would make a great pastor's wife. She loved someone else and became engaged to someone else and married that man. So my student concluded, "How can I lead a church to trust God for answers to prayer, if I can't get them?"

I brought him back to the negative and positive elements of First John 3:22. "Have you obeyed the word of God when you asked God for these things?"

"Yes," he tried to be honest when he answered.

But there's a second part of getting your prayers answered, "What have you done to please God?" Then I asked him about his faith, "Did you really believe God would do it when you asked?"

"No," he confessed his lack of deep faith in God.

I went on to point out he was blaming God for not answering his prayer when the problem could be his lack of faith. We talked quietly awhile about faith for ministry. He was afraid of failure in ministry and was looking for any loop hole to get out of it.

Let's Pray Now

There's a lot of blindness in our lives when it comes to obeying God and the things He wants us to do. After interviewing many leaders and "potential leaders," I find there is a lot of subjectivity in their obedience to God.

What do I mean by subjective obedience? Most obey what they want to obey, and they are blind to things they don't want to obey. As an illustration, some pastors honestly think they obey God explicitly and completely, but they are careless about winning souls. Lost people touch their lives every day and they make no effort to win them to Christ, nor do they use the resources of their church in evangelism.

As a result of their partial blindness, they may have a great church in one area, but they have not done awesome things by faith. I.e., partial blindness produces partially completed works for God.

There is a principle of *priority faith*, which suggests God has a set of priorities to guide the ministry of His leaders. Those leaders who give attention to God's highest priority accomplish the greatest church for God. When a church leader ministers toward the bottom of God's priority list, their church becomes a partially completed work for God, no matter the size, income, or the human measuring points.

The following order of *Faith Priorities* will help guide leaders to build a great, well-rounded work for God.

10 Priorities of Faith

What type of faith does God honor?

1. When believers establish an intimate relationship with God.

2. When believers worship God for Who He is (see John 4:29).

3. When believers love God and put Him first in their lives (see Matt. 22:37-39).

4. When believers attempt to evangelize the unsaved (see 2 Pet. 3:9).

5. When believers live holy lives that please the Lord (James 1:17 ELT).

6. When believers become actively involved in their local Body of Christ.

7. When believers carry out the commands of spiritual ministry to others.

8. When believers minister to the needy outside the Body of Christ.

9. When believers trust God to supply their necessities: food, clothing, and shelter.

10. When believers trust God for buildings, property, equipment, or stuff.

Also, look at your spiritual gifts when it comes to obeying God. Remember the parable of the owner who gave talents to his employees before going away. The owner gave one employee five talents, another two talents, and to the final employee he gave one talent. *"To every man according to his revealed ability"* (Matt. 25:15).

The first two workers were rewarded according to their faithfulness—obedience—but, the third did nothing with his one talent—disobedience. So it was taken from him. This suggests that one's faith was wrapped up in one's obedience to the owner in relationship to their talent. The owner didn't expect the worker with one talent to accomplish what the worker with five talents did. The owner expected obedience, or faithfulness to his task.

Each worker for God should do his or her best—complete obedience—so he or she will hear the Master say, *"Well done, good and faithful servant; you were faithful over a few things, I will make you ruler over many things..."* (Matt. 25:21).

6

Repentance Answers

*The Hezekiah Factor in Isaiah 38—Our Repentance of Sin
Re-establishes Fellowship with God and Brings about
God's Answer of Deliverance from Problems or Suffering*

HEZEKIAH, THE KING OF ISRAEL, got sick and was near death when Isaiah the prophet came to tell him, *"Set your house in order, for you shall die and not live"* (Isa. 38:1).

But what did Hezekiah do? He *"turned his face toward the wall and prayed to the Lord"* (Isa. 38:2). But it was not just praying, the Bible describes the intensity of his prayer, *"Hezekiah wept bitterly"* (Isa. 38:3).

The prayer of Hezekiah is written in Isaiah 38:10-17. In that he recognizes, *"For You [God] have cast all my sins behind Your back"* (Isa. 38:17). Because of his repentance and deep prayers, God came to him and said, *"I have heard your prayer, I have seen your tears; surely I will add to your life fifteen years"* (Isa. 38:5). He became the first man to know the date of his death. Other than that, only God controls the fate of our destiny and the day when we shall die. Hezekiah's repentance led to an additional 15 years to his life.

Hezekiah was a good king who lived a godly life. Even good people have to repent of secret sin or ignorant sin before God answers their prayers. On the other hand, there are evil people who must repent before their prayers are answered. Such was the case of Ahab: *"Ahab did more to provoke the Lord God of Israel to anger than all the kings of Israel who were before him"* (1 Kings 16:33).

On one occasion, King Ahab coveted Naboth's vineyard, his neighbor next to the palace. So Ahab's wife Jezebel plotted to murder Naboth to get the vineyard for Ahab. God saw the treachery of King Ahab and Queen Jezebel and spoke through the prophet Elijah, *"Have you murdered and also taken possession...Thus says the Lord, 'In the place where the dogs licked the blood of Naboth, dogs shall lick your* [Ahab's] *blood, even yours'"* (1 Kings 21:19). Then, God told Ahab that He would... *"take away your posterity and will cut off from Ahab every male in Israel, both bond and free"* (1 Kings 21:21). In this God said that He would wipe out the entire lineage of Ahab.

To Ahab's credit, he repented so deeply that God was touched to postpone the judgment on Ahab. *"When Ahab heard those words...he tore his clothes and put sackcloth on his body, and fasted and lay in sackcloth, and went about mourning"* (1 Kings 21:27).

God told Isaiah to deliver a second message to Ahab, *"...Because he has humbled himself before me, I will not bring the calamity in his days. In the days of his son I will bring the calamity on his house"* (1 Kings 21:29).

LET'S PRAY NOW

Sometimes God will not hear our prayers because of our sin, *"If I regard inequity in my heart, the Lord will not hear"* (Ps. 66:18). *"God does not hear sinners"* (John 9:31). And then, perhaps the most convicting verse of all, *"Behold, the Lord's hand is not shortened that it cannot save; nor his ear heavy* [plugged up with wax], *that it cannot hear. But your inequities have separated you from your God; and your sins have hidden His face from you so that He will not hear"* (Isa. 59:1-2).

"If we say that we have no sin [sin nature] *we deceive ourselves and the truth is not in us,"* (1 John 1:8). Therefore, we cannot say that we are purified from our sin nature. Also, *"If we say that we have not sinned* [the act of sin], *we make Him a liar, and His word is not in us"*

(1 John 1:10). So we have to deal with our sin to get God to answer our prayers.

How do we do that? If we confess or repent, God will hear and restore us. *"If we confess our sins, He is faithful and just to forgive us our sins and to cleanse us from all unrighteousness"* (1 John 1:9).

So before you intercede for lost people, or you ask for money, or you pray for healing, or any other prayer, make sure that first you are in fellowship with God and that every known sin in your life is covered by the blood of Christ. Then you can get answers to your prayers.

The Psalmist said, *"I acknowledged my sin to You, and my iniquity I have not hidden. I said, 'I will confess my transgressions to the Lord,' and You forgave the iniquity of my sin"* (Ps. 32:5).

If you're a Christian walking in fellowship with Christ, God will automatically forgive your sins based on the blood of Jesus Christ, *"If we walk in the light as He is in the light, we have fellowship one with another and the blood of Jesus Christ His Son cleanses us from all sin"* (1 John 1:7).

So are you on praying ground? If so, then pray.

7

Tarrying Answers

The Upper Room Factor—God Answers When
We Wait in His Presence for Our Answer

JESUS COMMANDED HIS DISCIPLES TO tarry in the Lord's presence to get what they needed from Him. *"Tarry in the city of Jerusalem until you are endued with power from on high"* (Luke 24:49). What did the disciples do? *"And when they had entered...the upper room...These all continued with one accord in prayer and supplication..."* (Acts 1:13-14).

Notice what happened because they tarried in prayer, *"When the Day of Pentecost had fully come, they were all with one accord in one place. And suddenly there came a sound from heaven, as of a rushing mighty wind, and it filled the whole house where they were sitting. Then there appeared to them divided tongues, as of fire, and one sat upon each of them. And they were all filled with the Holy Spirit and began to speak with other tongues..."* (Acts 2:1-4).

While this command to tarry in Jerusalem is a *descriptive command*, meaning it applied to certain disciples at a certain place for a certain purpose, it was not a *prescriptive command*, meaning all who go to Jerusalem to tarry in prayer today should not expect the same results as the disciples got in the upper room. (We can all expect to be filled with the Holy Spirit, but we should not expect actual tongues of fire to sit on our heads. That was a one-time historic event.)

However, the eternal principle of tarrying in prayer to get answers from God is still operative. We are told in the Old Testament, *"Wait on the Lord: be of good courage and He shall strengthen your heart: wait, I say, on the Lord"* (Ps. 27:14). Continually throughout the Book of Psalms, the Psalmist declares, *"I wait for You"* (Ps. 25:21; 69:3; 130:5).

I was saved because of a prayer meeting in Bonna Bella, Georgia, in the summer of 1950. Bill and Burt Hardin were twin brothers who were students at Columbia Bible College; but on the weekend they preached at Bonna Bella Presbyterian Church, in greater Savannah, Georgia. The old church had been there a long time, but had recently built a small new concrete block auditorium with aluminum windows, but not much else. But the twins were not interested in constructing a building; they were interested in winning people to Jesus Christ.

The Harding boys called for a prayer meeting every morning from 5 A.M. to 8 A.M. on the front porch of the garage apartment where they lived. It was a two-car garage, with rickety steps that led up to a screened porch and a one-room apartment. One twin met the people at 5 A.M. on the screened porch and prayed with intercessors until 6:30 A.M. The other twin led the meeting from 6:30 A.M. to 8 A.M. People were asked to come pray on their way to work each morning, but no one stayed the entire time.

I never attended this prayer meeting, and didn't know anything about it until the revival was over. The intercessors could not be called great prayer warriors, but their greatness was in their faithfulness and simple belief that God could do anything that they asked. They had a sheet of paper with approximately 60 names of unsaved high school students. Person after person would come to pray over that sheet of paper. Sometimes there was a gap between one person who prayed, before the next intercessor showed up. But in my mind I can hear them pray, "Save Elmer Towns...save Art Winn...save Ann Perry...save L. J. McEwen..."

The working people in that simple waterfront village interceded for a great miracle, and God heard and answered in a great way. God rewarded the faithful who continued in prayer.

During the last two weeks of July 1950, the twins invited Joel Ortendahl, a fellow student from Columbia Bible College (a Baptist) to come preach a revival meeting. It was then the power of God was poured out on that little church.

In the first service, Mr. and Mrs. Ernie Miller were converted, along with all five of their children. Mrs. Miller stood to give a testimony in the following meeting, "You all know me, I used to be a Jehovah's Witness, I went door to door witnessing for Jehovah, but now I've found that the real Jehovah is Jesus Christ my Lord, and I've been born again…."

Mrs. Miller then referred to her husband, who at this time was too shy to give a public testimony. She said, "My husband, Ernie, is a Jew and he has found out that the real Messiah is Jesus Christ. He's been born again."

The testimony of the Miller family spread like wild-fire throughout the community. People couldn't believe the transformation because they remembered Mrs. Miller going door-to-door as a Jehovah Witness. So multitudes came to the church to see and hear what God was doing. Every night there were four or five saved, some nights as many as ten or eleven. Not great numbers in sight of the history of revivals, but the numbers in Bonna Bella were staggering to those who lived there.

On about the fourth night of the revival, a man went forward to receive Jesus Christ as Savior. After the invitation was over, he stood to testify, "All of you folks know me, I'm your (rural) mail man." He told how he delivered the mail to almost everybody in the room, and could tell their name and box number. Then he explained, "As I came down Laroach Avenue, I began to feel heat coming from this building. The closer I got, the hotter my face felt. Not until I passed the church building did the heat go away. Then I decided I had to come and see what was happening for myself."

This experience has been called *atmospheric revival*, where the presence of God is poured out among His people (see Joel 2:28), so individuals experience the presence of God. Just as one feels water in the air before it begins raining, so you can feel the presence of God when His Spirit is poured out on a meeting.

Then the postman declared, "I was baptized in a Baptist church when I was a boy, I've been a deacon, Sunday school teacher, and usher in a Baptist church, but I've never been born again. Tonight I asked Christ to come into my heart and I have been born again."

Great revival was poured out in Bonna Bella Presbyterian Church because a group of intercessors tarried in prayer for those 60 young people whose names were typed on a sheet of paper. Most of those whose names were on that paper went forward to receive Jesus Christ as their Savior.

July 25, 1950, was a crucial night. No one came forward; Bill Harding went down and stood in front of the communion table to say,

"Someone here has been touched by God tonight, and you're supposed to come forward to get saved, but you're hanging on to the pew in front of you." I looked down and saw my white knuckles wrapped around the pew and immediately let go. Bill continued,

"I want you to go home, kneel by your bed, look into Heaven and say, 'Lord, I've never done it before; Jesus come into my heart and save me.'"

That night I did what Bill Hardin told me and I was born again and forever transformed.

LET'S PRAY NOW

Some fast and pray for 40 days in a secluded place. Others for 10 days, and many just tarry in fasting and prayer for one day. The issue is not the length of time, but your heart condition before God. The sincerity of your request will get an answer from God, not the length of time. But if you're really sincere, you'll stay as long as necessary to get your answer from God.

If you're going to tarry, find a suitable spot and stay there in prayer as long as necessary. Some will remain for a designated time until they get an answer. Others will designate a specific time, and come back to that spot for prayer time and again. Their length for tarrying is not in one long period of time, but rather repeated times of prayer over a longer stretch of time.

8

Two-Pray Answers

*The Matthew 18:19 Factor: God Answers
When Two People Agree and Pray Together
for the Request They Both Want from God*

WHEN YOU THINK OF GOD answering *two-pray*, think of Paul and Silas in prison having been beaten and locked in the stocks. In the middle of the night, *"Paul and Silas were praying and singing hymns"* (Acts 16:25). God sent an earthquake to open the gates and release them from prison.

Two-pray reminds us of Moses praying for victory over the Amalekites in Exodus 17. When his arms became tired and he couldn't continue interceding, he dropped his arms and the Amalekites began winning the battle. It took two people—Hur and Aaron—to hold his arms to continue intercession, *"And Aaron and Hur supported his hands, one on one side, and the other on the other side...so Joshua defeated Amalek"* (Exod. 17:12-13).

One of the most amazing promises in the Bible is that God will hear and answer your prayer when you ask in agreement with another person. *"Again I say to you that if two of you agree on earth concerning anything that they ask, it will be done for them by My Father in heaven"* (Matt. 18:19).

The word "agree" comes from *sumphunes*, the word from which we get "symphony." Think of how all the instruments of an orchestra come together in a harmonious, beautiful sound, a sound agreeable to you even though many at the same time are playing different notes on different sounding instruments. That's the way it is with prayer; when many people pray about the same thing together, yet using many different words, with many different passions, and approaching God in many different ways, it's beautiful in God's ear.

God has a weakness for unity among His people. When His people come together in agreement, God listens and hears their prayers. I wrote *Prayer Partners*[1] to motivate Christians to pray with other people to get answers from God. Technically, it's a process I now call *two-pray*.

In 1992 I had read C. Peter Wagner's book *Prayer Shield* [2] in its typed form, because Peter had asked me to write a recommendation for his book. I took the highlighted copy into my early Sunday morning prayer meeting at Thomas Road Baptist Church and read some important sections to the intercessors with whom I prayed. Then I asked one of the most important questions in my life:

"Will you make my ministry your prayer ministry?"

That question seemed to be extremely egotistical in that I was asking them to join me as partners and pray for my needs and ministry. Yet God had put the question upon my heart, and I was looking for prayer partners in ministry. I felt I could do what they couldn't do: write books, speak to pastor groups, and teach university classes; but they had a prayer ministry in a way that I couldn't have (others can intercede for you in a way you can't pray for yourself). Then I cautioned the people not to answer me that day, but to pray about it one week and see if God burdened their heart.

My number one prayer partner is Buddy Bryant, a logger who cuts timber in the woods of Central Virginia to take to the paper mills of Virginia, or the woodworking factories of North Carolina. Buddy told me, "I get up at four o'clock every morning, and pray until five. That's when I pray for you." Then he goes to work and when the other loggers are listening to loud rock and roll music on their earphones—because power saws are deafening—Buddy uses earplugs so he can pray while cutting timber in the woods.

On January 6, 2008, I was supposed to preach at Morningside Church in Port St. Lucie, Florida, but the night before I came down with a terrible case of flu, vomiting, and diarrhea. I passed out several times in my motel room because I was so weak. Later that afternoon, I was still weak and nauseous when the pastor left me at the West Palm Beach Airport to fly home to Lynchburg. I was barely making it when it came time to change planes in Charlotte, North Carolina. The plane I was supposed to catch had a mechanical failure and a 2-3 hour delay was posted. That would place me getting home past midnight. I was afraid of passing out in the airport and ending up in the emergency room of some hospital in Charlotte.

I began to pray for something to happen, and then I thought of Buddy. I called him on my cell phone, and he answered, "Usually, I'm asleep by this time, but for some reason I couldn't go to sleep." When I told him of my predicament, he immediately broke into prayer over the phone for my healing, as well as for the plane to leave immediately.

After Buddy prayed, I agreed with him in prayer for the same thing: asking for healing and for God to get me home as soon as possible.

Almost immediately, after hanging up, I saw an aircraft tug pulling an airplane up to the gate and heard the announcement, "Another plane is here and we will be leaving within twenty minutes; don't leave the gate area…."

There was a young man sitting next to me who had overheard my conversation with Buddy, including my prayer. He said in a skeptical manner, "I bet you think that airplane is an answer to your prayer." Then he went on to explain, "That's not a miracle, just coincidence."

I really didn't want to answer him, because I was feeling so rotten, so I prayed for God to give me an answer and said, "I serve a God of coincidences…."

The young man shrugged his shoulders and walked away. I never got to talk to him, but I've often prayed for God to use this story of "coincidental answer" that God gave to me that evening.

I accidentally stumbled onto the secret of *two-pray* as I was teaching the Pastor's Bible Class at Thomas Road Baptist Church in 1986. I began praying *with* members of my class, rather than just praying *for* them. I had a large class (attendance averaged approximately 1,000 at the time). I didn't know how to keep up with that many people, especially because there were so many absentees. It is easy for people to fall between the cracks. So I divided up the auditorium in sections; I placed section leaders over people who sat together in the same section of pews. I asked these section leaders to phone absentees in their section to encourage them to return the next Sunday.

Because I wouldn't ask workers to do what I was unwilling to do, each week I made about five to ten absentee phone calls. Here, unknowingly, I stumbled onto the power of *two-pray*. Here's how my phone conversation usually went:

"Hello, this is Dr. Towns calling from class...."

Usually they greeted me back; most of the time they were surprised that I would take the initiative to phone them. I never asked, "Why were you absent?" Here's what I said next:

"I missed you last Sunday, and in a large class it's very easy for people to fall between the cracks." I assured them of my love and concern, then I asked,

"How may I pray for you?"

Little did I know that my question would open up great opportunities for spiritual ministries. They began opening up to tell me their deepest problems. They told me about sicknesses in their family, or about being laid off from their job, or their wife left them, or their husband beat them, or their husband was in jail, or their children had run away from home. I did not put them off with the promise, "I'll pray for you." My response was immediate,

"Let's pray about it now...over the phone...." Before I prayed, I would ask another question, "What do you want God to do about this?"

I discovered what I intended to pray was not always the same thing they wanted. One time a middle-aged daughter told me her elderly mother was sick and near death. I responded, "Let's ask God to heal her." The daughter replied quickly, "Oh no! She's too far gone, her body organs are not functioning." The daughter asked that her mother might die without pain.

So find out from the people what they want God to do; that's asking them to make a statement of faith. Then the two of you can agree specifically for that request. This means two are "agreeing" in prayer together.

You get answers by doing two things: first, you must agree with your prayer partners before you ask; and second, you must ask together. That's all! If you will do these two things, you will become *much more successful* in praying.

LET'S PRAY NOW

Why does God promise to answer prayers when two people agree? Obviously, God wants more than a "speaking" agreement, because two people repeating the same words is not *agree-pray*. They can say the same words, but their hearts may be going in different directions. God wants two people to agree in *vision-pray*…agree in *faith-pray*…agree in *insight-pray*…and agree in *spirit-pray*.

Since the word *agree* suggests *harmony* in the original language, then God is impressed when two people *harmony-pray*. Why does God like us to harmonize in prayer? Because we become responsible to one another. We must search our hearts in the presence of our partners to make sure there are no hindrances. We each strive to get as close to God as possible and when we pray together, each agrees with the passion and sincerity of the other.

And because responsibility leads to accountability, we each realize that the other person is examining us, just as God examines us. We are *eavesdropping* on their conversation with God, so to speak. As we join in with their prayers, we become one in spirit, as we agree in prayer.

Then just as accountability leads to productivity in the business world, the same happens in the spiritual world; God answers our prayers knowing "we are one heart before God."

- Responsibility—we pray better
- pray honestly
- pray biblically

ENDNOTES

1. The entire book may be found on my Website: www.elmertowns.com. Click on Books; the book may be read or downloaded free.

2. C. Peter Wagner, *Prayer Shield* (Ventura, CA: Regal Books, 1992).

9

Vision Answers

God Gives You a Vision of How the Answer Can Come for Which One Prays

WHAT DOES THE MAN OF God do when he has a directive from God to plant a church, yet he has no money to purchase land and the land that is available costs a million dollars an acre? God answered with a vision of how it could be done.

Dave Earley, a 1985 Liberty University graduate was beginning a church in the greater Columbus, Ohio, area— New Life Community Church, Gahanna, Ohio (average attendance now 2,000 people). Every desirable site he looked at cost over a million dollars an acre. Dave felt God was leading in a different way.

When I went to organize the two-month-old congregation, we left the junior high building, where services were being held, around 1 P.M. after the morning service was over.

"I want to show you something," Dave said to me, explaining, "I want your opinion."

We stopped near a bridge of a small winding stream through low marsh land covered with trees and bushes. Technically, it was a flood plain. "It only costs $50,000," David explained.

"We can build our church on one side of the creek and park cars on the other side," Dave explained. Then he described moving dirt from the higher edge of the ten acres to the center and straightening out the creek.

"Dave, that's a swamp!" I said emphatically.

"But I can do it," Dave explained.

"Dave, it's a swamp," I kept saying.

The man of God can see a vision to do what no one else thinks can be done. He can look at his problems and see a new way…as a better way…or God's way to solve the problem that's keeping him from going forward.

Five years later Jerry Falwell and I flew to Columbus to dedicate the first sanctuary of New Life Community Baptist Church that seated 450 people. The place was packed. Jerry preached the dedication sermon and I told the people the story,

"It's a swamp."

Everyone laughed. They had parked their cars on a paved parking lot that had been located on one side of the creek, and they were sitting in a sanctuary that was constructed in what I had called a "swamp." It was a laugh of faith!

In 1995—the church was ten years old—Jerry and I flew again to dedicate a 1,000-seat auditorium on that same ten acres of flood plain. Again Jerry preached and I told the story, "It's a swamp." Again, they rejoiced with me by a laugh of faith.

The man of God can do extraordinary things when God honors his faith by giving him a vision of how his prayers can be answered.

LET'S PRAY NOW

Sometimes God answers your prayers by showing you how to answer your own prayers in a different way from the thing you requested from Him. God can bring circumstances together in a way that's different from what you prayed (called *circumstantial answers*).

Sometimes God tells us to wait before He answers. Maybe conditions are not yet ready. Maybe it takes time for God to send the thing for which you're praying. If you pray for your newborn son to be a track star, God will say, "Wait…20 years."

Maybe you pray for your child to be a great Christian worker. You may have to wait to see the answer, but God may give you an inner assurance that it will happen. That's a *vision answer*.

Moses sinned publicly when he struck the rock at Meribah instead of speaking to the rock. He was punished. *"Because you did not believe Me, to hallow Me in the eyes of the children of Israel, therefore you shall not bring this assembly into the land…"* (Num. 20:12). Yet before Moses died he went to the top of Mount Nebo where *"the Lord showed him all the land of Gilead as far as Dan"* (Deut. 34:1). That's a *vision answer*.

10

Yielding Answers

The Daniel Factor: God Answers When
We Yield to Do His Will

D ANIEL AND HIS THREE FRIENDS—Shadrach, Meshach, and Abed-Nego—were all taken captive to the city of Babylon in 606 B.C. When Nebuchadnezzar surrounded Jerusalem and threatened to destroy it, Israel gave great amounts of treasure to the Babylonian king, and promised to send taxes—more treasures—each year. Also, a number of young Israelites were sent to Babylon to be trained in the Babylonian way of doing business so they could become civil servants to carry out the duties of Babylon in Israel.

Daniel and the three young men were among those young Israelites sent to Babylon. They were probably placed in dormitories when they arrived and assigned to "eat" at the king's tables, which meant they ate out of the kitchen that supplied the king's food.

"But Daniel purposed in his heart that he would not defile him-self with the portion of the king's delicacies…" (Daniel 1:8).

Why did Daniel not want to eat the king's food? It could be: (1) it violated Jewish ceremonial law, (2) it had been offered to foreign idols, or (3) it was alcohol-related and would numb his senses. Daniel suggested to his overseer *"a ten-day diet of only vegetables and water"* (Dan. 1:12 TLB).

Daniel was willing to put God on the spot. When he suggested that they prove him and his three young friends, Daniel did not say he would eat their food if their health failed, nor did Daniel say they could punish him if their health failed, nor did it say they could kill him if their health failed. Daniel put God first and yielded to God's will.

There was a second test for Daniel's three friends. Apparently Daniel was away and not present, but the three friends—Shadrach, Meshach, and Abed-Nego—were compelled to bow before a statue, probably an idol representative of King Nebuchadnezzar who was to be treated as a god.

The young men refused to bow down to the idol. They yielded themselves to God saying, *"If it be so, our God whom we serve is able to deliver us from the burning fiery furnace"* (Dan. 3:17 KJV). But then the boys were level-headed, they understood the consequences when they yielded to God, *"But if not"* (Dan. 3:18 KJV). In that statement, the three young men realized that God may not deliver them and were willing to die for their convictions. They said, *"But if not, let it be known to you, O king, that we do not serve your gods, nor will we worship the gold image which you have set up"* (Dan. 3:18).

The story is well known that God protected the young men when they were thrown into the fiery furnace.

When King Nebuchadnezzar looked into the furnace, *"Look!"* he answered, *"I see four men loose, walking in the midst of the fire; and they are not hurt, and the form of the fourth is like the Son of God"* (Dan. 3:25).

Nebuchadnezzar realized that these were different young men, different from all the others he had captured. Then he realized why they were different, because they had *"yielded their bodies, that they might not serve nor worship any god except their own God"* (Dan. 3:18 ELT). We, like these three young men, must yield everything to God to get our prayers answered.

LET'S PRAY NOW

Yieldedness is one of the keys to answered prayer. If God has not answered your prayer, then you ought to search your heart, for there might be something that is unyielded to God.

Because sin is so deceptive, and we are spiritually blinded (2 Cor. 4:3-4), we need to pray for illumination that we might see any sin in our lives that we may not normally see. Paul prayed for the spiritual enlightenment of the Ephesians that *"the eyes of your understanding being enlightened; that you may know what is the hope of His calling, what are the riches of the glory of His inheritance in the saints, and what is the exceeding greatness of His power toward us who believe, according to the working of His mighty power"* (Eph. 1:18-19).

Some people are like Jonah; they refuse to do God's will, and they even run in the opposite direction. God must punish them as He did Jonah when a great fish swallowed him. It is only then that some will yield to God—as did Jonah—and only then do they go and do God's will.

So even before you begin to yield yourself to God, pray for spiritual illumination to see the areas that you are hiding from God. And in your prayer, you may find things hidden from you so that you don't realize there is danger in your heart.

There are many homeowners who have termites, but they never realize it until a pest inspection reveals the termite infestation is present. Then the workers can apply chemicals to remove the termites. In the same way, we sometimes need an inspection by the Holy Spirit to find out what in our hearts is keeping our prayers from being answered.

Paul tells us, *"Yield yourselves unto God, as those that are alive from the dead"* (Rom. 6:13 KJV). In the moment of spiritual yieldedness, we find life and peace.

SECTION

THE REALLY
HARD ANSWERS

11

Healing Answers

When God Supernaturally Heals

CHARLES HUGHES WAS AN OUTSTANDING upperclassman at Liberty University who was called into evangelism. God's power had rested upon him, for he preached in some of the largest churches in America (over 5,000 in attendance) and had great results in souls saved, yet he was still an undergraduate at Liberty University.

Charles was traveling to an evangelistic crusade in Harrisburg, Pennsylvania, in 1978 when the van in which he was riding was hit by an eighteen-wheeler semi and was completely demolished. Charles' head was crushed and to save his life the doctors removed the top of his skull because of intense internal swelling of the brain.

After doing everything possible, the doctors told Jerry Falwell and his father, Dr. Robert Hughes, Dean of Liberty Theological Seminary, that Charles would die. The doctors asked the family if they would sign papers to donate his organs to living recipients. The medical community felt that Charles was as good as dead.

When faced with this emergency, Falwell called a day of fasting and prayer by the entire ministry family of Liberty University and Thomas Road Baptist Church. Some advised Jerry not to do it because Charles was "as good as dead."

But Jerry believed prayer and fasting would save Charles' life. The following night at Thomas Road Baptist Church auditorium Jerry announced, "I am so sure that Charles will be healed, that I am inviting him to be the speaker at Liberty's graduation this year." At that time, graduation was only five months away, and Charles was hanging on to a faint sliver of life.

Sometimes God gives an inner assurance—supernatural faith—that He's about to do something great. This is called *"the prayer of faith that will save the sick"* (James 5:15). A prayer of faith is being absolutely sure the answer will come before it happens.

Five months later, Charles sat on the platform with Jerry Falwell, a huge bandage around his head. The day's greatest miracle was Charles himself, not the results of the message that he was going to bring. Sadly, much of the power that Charles had as a young man was lost. His message was average, but everyone present agreed that the greatest miracle that day was that Charles was alive. The event was electrified. God honored the faith of the entire Thomas Road Baptist Church family and Liberty student body. Today, Charles has gone on to earn his bachelor's, master's, and doctorate degrees.

And what does Charles do today for ministry? He is in charge of the Prayer Room at Liberty University. He doesn't have to say much to encourage students to pray; just his life in the Prayer Room is a testimony to all that "God answers prayers."

LET'S PRAY NOW

When you begin to pray for someone who needs healing, examine whether they are sick because of sin in their life. Notice the promise of healing is attached to the condition of confessing sin and getting forgiveness, *"The prayer of faith shall save the sick...and if he has committed sins he will be forgiven,* [therefore] *confess your trespasses"* (James 5:15-16). Why does the Bible connect sickness to sin? For two reasons: First, because certain sins cause physical illness. We know that cigarette smoking leads to cancer, and excessive alcohol drinking leads to cirrhosis of the liver, and a sexually filthy lifestyle can lead to AIDS. Therefore, sin can be the direct cause of a person's illness, or it can be an indirect cause through circumstances that bring about illness—sin destroys a person's self-discipline and/or cleanliness, so that a filthy lifestyle introduces germs and infections into the body. Second, their illness is a judgment of God. On another occasion, *"Many are weak and sick among you..."* (1 Cor. 11:30).

So the sick person must deal with their sins for healing. Notice again the passage says, *"Confess your trespasses one to another...that you may be healed"* (James 5:16). Sins must be dealt with before God will administer healing.

James introduced the section on praying for sick people by pointing us to the consequences of sin, *"lest you fall into judgment"* (James 5:12).

The elders of the church must be involved in praying for healing. James tells us, *"...call for the elders..."* (James 5:14). Why elders and not a traveling evangelist, or some other person? Because elders have spiritual oversight of the flock of God, and they probably know of any sin or rebellion in the life of the sick person that led to his or her illness. Because elders have the command to *"shepherd the flock"* (1 Peter 5:2), they must know their flock to exercise "watch-care" over their flock, and pray for those in their flock. Therefore, based on their spiritual relationship to the sick person, they can provide healing for the soul before they provide prayer for the body. Perhaps many who have prayed for healing didn't get it because they left out the ministry of their local church.

When you pray for healing, you are asking God to give the person spiritual and physical life. Remember, the Bible teaches, *"Every good gift and every perfect gift is from above,"* (James 1:17). Therefore, it is God who gives good health.

Good health comes from God, but it also comes from the body. The body has the ability to heal itself. A doctor, medicine, or any other therapy doesn't really heal the person. The body heals itself. A doctor may prescribe a medicine to eliminate a cause of illness— germs, infections, or other causal factors. Also a doctor may cut away infection in surgery. But in the final analysis, the body heals itself. So when you pray for someone's healing, you're praying for something the body is already trying to do—get well.

When you pray for healing, you should also ask God to reveal any unknown or unseen factors that cause sickness. Maybe a doctor has not made the patient any better. Maybe there's something that causes a person to be sick that hasn't been treated. Your responsibility is to pray for insight to discover what caused the illness.

When I was teaching at Trinity Evangelical Divinity School in the late '60s, I had a colleague who became very sick and the medical community was unable to discover the cause of the illness. But after a day or two in the hospital, he got well and went back to work.

This happened a couple of times, and only when he was hospitalized did he get better.

Then the entire family came down with the same symptoms, they stopped praying for healing, and began asking God to reveal the unseen cause of their physical problems. Shortly thereafter, they discovered that a beautiful set of China cups that had been given to them had not been thoroughly fired in a kiln to seal the ceramic finish. The lead paint melted in the hot tea, and they were unknowingly poisoning themselves. So how did God heal the family? By helping them discover the cause of their sickness.

Pray for God to effectively use the drugs and/or therapy described by the physician. The same with exercise and physical therapy. Pray for the revitalization of the body when therapy is used.

Don't be discouraged if God doesn't answer your prayer for healing. It's not God's will that everyone be healed. Remember, Paul prayed three times for God to take away his *"thorn in the flesh,"* but God didn't answer that request (2 Cor. 12:8). Also, Paul said he left Trophimus sick in Miletum (2 Tim. 4:20). Even Jesus didn't heal every sick person He met. He encountered a great multitude at the Pool of Bethesda (see John 5:3), but He only healed one man who had been lame for 38 years (see John 5:5-9). On another occasion, Jesus cured all who came to see Him (see Matt. 12:15), but on another occasion, *"they brought to Him **all** who were sick"* and *"He healed **many** who were sick with various diseases"* (Mark 1:32, 34, emphasis added). Did you see that *all* were brought, but He healed only *many*? That suggests Jesus did not heal all.

Finally, the key to healing is not your faith, nor is it the severity of the sick person. Healing power is with God. When you exercise the "prayer of faith," remember it is faith in the source of healing— God—that you must recognize, not faith in your prayer, or even faith in your faith. You must have faith in what God can do. Since God can do all things, God can heal anyone. But since God doesn't do everything that is asked of Him, but He only does His will; then let's pray in the will of God. Let's pray *"not My will, but Yours be done"* (Luke 22:42).

12

Interventional Answers

When We Want God to Remove a Serious Barrier to His
Work or Provide a Miraculous Supply of Resources

PRAYING FOR $35 MILLION

IN 1998 I WAS SITTING in a planning committee meeting for Billy Graham's training committee called *Amsterdam 2000*. Billy planned to bring together 10,000 evangelists from 235 nations of the earth. While all would be asked to pay their own expenses, most of them could not attend without significant subsidy. The conference would raise funds to help to pay their expenses to Amsterdam, Netherlands, including airfare, food, and accommodations for 10 days.

"I want to train them to do evangelism, just like I do it," Billy said to the 16 of us through John Corts, the Executive Director of the Billy Graham Evangelistic Association. So we were seeking to invite only evangelists who proclaim the good news of Christ, urge a personal response to Christ, and provide nurture to incorporate new believers into local church fellowships.

Billy said, "My greatest legacy is not a school of evangelism with my name on it, but to have 10,000 evangelists doing soul-winning the way I understand evangelism, but doing it in their own native tongue within their cultural expressions of their native home."

Previously, Billy had organized *Amsterdam '83* for 3,000 participants and *Amsterdam '86* for another 6,000 itinerant evangelists. It had cost $35 million. Now, 13 years later we were planning to train 10,000 more evangelists and there had been 13 years of inflation. But after skillful planning and careful budgeting that incorporated what was learned from previous mistakes and experience, the committee felt it could put on *Amsterdam 2000* for the same per person cost of $3,500, or $35 million for 10,000 participants.

I choked at the amount because I am not a great man of faith.

I knew how hard it was to raise money—mass mailings, radio appeals, pledge cards, myriad phone calls, visits, and contacts, repeating the story, and asking for contributions. I thought to myself, "It's not easy to raise thirty-five million dollars. I've never seen Jerry Falwell go after that much money."

Then we were told, "Billy said, 'It'll be easy.'" The opposite of what I thought.

"I'll write and ask thirty-five thousand people to give me $1,000 each." He went on to explain, "There are about that many people who have, over the years, each given $1,000 or more to the Billy Graham Evangelistic Association."

Then he added, "It may be as simple as writing a letter to 35,000 people and trusting God to touch their hearts and enable them to support the vision."

Then I impulsively raised my hand, "I'll give the first $1,000."

What was insurmountable to me was a simple faith statement to Billy Graham. He believed God could supply millions of dollars because it included carrying out the call of God upon his life. Billy believed God could provide $35 million because it would lead to winning souls to Christ.

LET'S PRAY NOW

It's all right to ask for big extraordinary things, but make sure the thing for which you ask is God's will. Search your heart to make sure you are not asking for selfish reasons, or for your ease, riches, or glory. You must ask for things that are the will of God.

First, you must have confidence that *your prayers are based on God's will*. *"This is confidence…that if we ask according to His will He hears us, and we know when He hears us, we have the answers we seek of Him"* (1 John 5:14-15 ELT). You find God's will in God's Word. Sometimes it is God's will that a person dies just as it may be God's will for you to fail so He can lead you in another direction. Paul prayed three times for healing but didn't get it (see 2 Cor. 12:8-9).

Second, you must *be careful not to ask something that God has not promised in His Word.* Jesus tells us, *"If you abide in Me, and My words abide in you, you will ask what you desire, and it shall be done for you"* (John 15:7).

According to this verse, there are three things that get your prayers answered: (1) you must be abiding in Jesus, which means you have yielded yourself to Him, (2) God's Word must control your thinking and asking, and (3) you must ask to receive. Therefore, your prayers will be answered when you ask for things promised by the Bible.

Third, you must *tie your request to fasting and continual prayer.* Jesus said, *"…if you have faith…you will say to this mountain… move…and it will move…. However, this kind does not go out except by prayer and fasting"* (Matt. 17:20-21).

Can we really expect God to respond if we don't invest an enormous amount of time and agony in prayer? Just making a bold request doesn't move mountains.

So what must we do? We must make bold *faith requests* from the very depths of our beings. We must pray with all our hearts, giving up sleep for an all-night prayer meeting. We must fast and pray for a day, or for a week, or for 40 days. We must sacrifice because we know God *can* answer and we must keep praying until God *does* answer.

A casual request rolling off our tongues doesn't move God; but God responds when we pray so diligently that we cry and weep. So let me ask, when's the last time you begged God for something?

Fourth, because *we know God can answer, we never quit.* We keep praying even when everything seems black. A strong, bold *faith request* is not something we pray once and then forget. No! When our faith tells us that the answer will come, we can't quit. We ask for it when we get up in the morning and when we pray at a meal. We ask for it while driving around our city, and we ask for it right before we go to sleep. We keep praying, because we believe in a personal God who is guiding us to make extraordinary requests.

The fifth principle is **not doubting in the dark what God has shown us in the light.** The condition for answers is to *"not doubt in his heart...he will have whatever he says"* (Mark 11:23). We can't work up confidence in the flesh. Neither does it come from circumstances. Confidence comes from God who has the ability to answer.

13

Intimacy Answers

Whether Our Prayers Are Answered or Not, the Result Is That We Know God More Intimately

ONE OF THE MOST DIFFICULT answers to receive is when you pray to become more intimate with God. Note how John the Baptist prayed, *"He must increase, but I must decrease"* (John 3:30). Jesus said of all the men ever born, John the Baptist was the greatest, *"Among those born of women there has not risen one greater than John the Baptist"* (Matt. 11:11). Therefore, God must have answered his prayer for intimacy.

This means John the Baptist had more faith than Abraham, who is known for his faith. And John the Baptist had more courage than Elijah, who was the bold prophet. And John the Baptist had more wisdom than Solomon, who was the wisest of all men. And John the Baptist had more intimacy with God than David who was a man after God's own heart. Simply put, John the Baptist was the most outstanding believer that ever walked this earth.

John the Baptist, who is the greatest spiritual giant of all time, tells us what to pray to become more like Christ, *"He must increase, but I must decrease"* (John 3:30).

Can God answer your prayer for intimacy, and can you become the greatest Christian of all time? Can you become greater than John the Baptist? Notice Jesus' answer to that question, *"But he who is least in the kingdom of heaven is greater than he* [John the Baptist]*"* (Matt. 11:11). So, yes! You *can* become the greatest Christian of all times. But the answer is not the way you pray, but the heart attitude by which you pray. The answer is a negative prayer, "I must decrease." You must pray for humility. That's tough to ask for and tough to get. We are naturally throne-sitters; we don't like to make God or anyone else number one—we like sitting on the throne of our lives.

I've always been very slow to ask God for humility or patience because the Bible explains, *"The testing of your faith produces patience"* (James 1:3). I've felt if I prayed for patience, God would send me trials to make me more patient or more humble. But trials hurt and squeeze the joy out of life. Who wants misery? That's why I call this a difficult prayer.

Yes! The most difficult prayer in life is to become nothing, or to decrease in any area of our lives. Why? Because at the very heart and core of each of us is a consuming desire to "feed our ego"—love me, protect me, exalt me, and accept me. It's hard for our inner selves to pray against ourselves.

Our passion cries out for love, so it's hard to pray for God to take away the love we get from people. We all want more.

And all of us want to be number one; our great passion is to "exalt me." So, it's hard to pray for God to make us less important.

Then don't forget social acceptance we all desire, "accept me." We want to be one of the gang, so it's hard to pray for God to decrease our social acceptance.

And finally, we all desire "protect me"; we don't want anyone treading on our reputation or taking away our things or money. So it's hard to pray for any decrease in these areas.

It seems *"me"* is at the core of everything I do. How can I pray for "me" to decrease? That's a hard prayer!

So why is intimacy with God one of the most difficult answers to get? Because intimacy involves dying that Christ may live in us. Didn't Jesus say, *"Except a corn of wheat fall into the ground and die, it abideth alone: but if it die, it bringeth forth much fruit"* (John 12:24 KJV). When we learn to die to selfish things, we begin to live for God. But that's hard.

Paul reminded us that our spiritual death is a daily struggle when he said; *"I die daily"* (1 Cor. 15:31). None of us want to die at any time; we fight and struggle to stay alive. So the prayer of intimacy to decrease, or to "die" is the most difficult of all prayers to get answered.

We love the world and we love to live our own lives at our own pace. Did you get that "you" and "I" are at the center? Everything in our earthly lives revolves around our selfish existence. When the world says "watch out for number one," the Christian realizes number one may keep him from intimacy with God.

How can we say "Jesus first" when it's love me, exalt me, protect me, accept me? Paul told us his desire was to glory *"in the cross of our Lord Jesus Christ, by whom the world is crucified to me, as I to the world"* (Gal. 6:14). So Paul's prayer to die must have been effective. He had to be crucified to do all the things he did.

LET'S PRAY NOW

Remember, this is praying for spiritual death, not physical death. You can't do anything in the flesh to please God. You can't flog yourself to death, as did some medieval monks who tried to answer their own prayers with whips. You can't starve yourself to death, or isolate yourself to death, nothing like that.

Crucifixion is not something you do; it's something God does. As a matter of fact, Jesus has already done it. You must learn to experience death by allowing Christ to live in your life. *"I have been crucified with Christ, nevertheless I live, yet not I, but Christ liveth in me"* (Gal.. 2:20 ELT). Notice the past tense action; your death with Christ has already happened. So now you must act on that historical reality. You must die to selfish expressions today, because Christ died on Calvary.

To be intimate with God, you must arrive at the place Paul described: *"those who are Christ's have crucified the flesh with its passions and desires"* (Gal. 5:24). You don't get intimacy with God just by praying to be intimate. You must give up the sins of the flesh, so that you die to them. You do that by yielding, or giving up, or surrendering to God. You do that by quitting sin. You pray, "Lord, I'll not do it anymore." As you give up the lust of the flesh, you'll find the intimacy of God you seek.

Hallelujah—Christ has done it all. But remember, it's hard to die, both for you and for Christ. It was hard for Christ, who prayed, *"Let this cup pass from me"* (Matt. 26:39). Since Jesus found it hard to die, so will you. You'll hang on to your egotistical pride, and you won't let go of your filthy dreams. It's hard to die, that's why this section of the book is about hard-to-get answers.

Ask Christ to help you surrender the old life. He will. Then you'll learn that the hardest prayers to get answered have some of the sweetest answers ever.

14

Intuitive Direction Answers

When God Answers by Telling Us Intuitively What to Do

GEORGE PROVINSE GREW UP WITH my wife in Hope Congregational Church, St. Louis, Missouri, and during World War II he was a member of an Air Force bomber crew that made bombing raids over Nazi Germany. One night his plane was shot down and George parachuted to safety somewhere over Germany.

Hope Congregational Church was an Independent Bible church filled with people who believed that God heard prayers and supernaturally intervened. After the war was over and George returned home, individuals were able to trace the time of his bailing out of a burning airplane over Germany to the identical time when a group of ladies came together in the church to intercede for their servicemen in action (because of the faithful intercession of the ladies of this church, not a single serviceman from Hope Church was killed during WWII).

As George floated to the ground, he wondered where he would land. All he could see was the dark earth rushing toward him. He was wondering if it was the ocean, or a lake, or woods, or what. All he could say was, "God, help me!"

George landed safely in an open field and intuitively he knew what to do. Quickly he gathered his parachute, wrapping it into a ball; he knew he had to hide the parachute. If the Germans found the parachute, they would send dogs to hunt him down. Almost immediately he found a pile of rocks in the field, and hid his chute out of sight.

George listened for sounds of life; by this time the airplanes were gone and there was silence. No sound of cars, barking dogs; nothing but silence. Also, there were no lights in any direction. His impulse was to find trees or bushes and hide from view. But he was in a wide-open field. Looking in each direction, he saw nothing, so he began walking into the wind. "I've got to find a hiding place."

Suddenly he stopped. Something intuitively told him to stop and lay down on the ground. Not knowing why he had to obey, George Provinse lay on the ground, and eventually went to sleep. Back home in St. Louis on that fateful night, a group of ladies had gathered to pray for their servicemen, and specifically, God had placed upon their hearts to pray for George Provinse.

When daylight came, George found himself approximately 15 feet from the edge of a steep cliff. If he had wandered blindly on in the evening, he would have fallen over the cliff, perhaps to his death. There was no reason for him to stop and lie down, neither was it logical nor did he have any other inclination to stop. It was just an inner thing that he knew he had to do.

There are times in the lives of Christians when God directs them through their inner radar screen; God wants them to stop... go...turn...and all the believer can do is obey the inner prompting of God.

Philip the evangelist was in the Gaza territory south of Jerusalem when he saw an Ethiopian in a chariot reading aloud from the Book of Isaiah to his entourage. When Philip saw this group of people, the Holy Spirit said, *"Go near and overtake this chariot"* (Acts 8:29). Did the Holy Spirit speak aloud to Philip? Did the Holy Spirit speak inwardly, or did Philip actually hear the inner voice of the Spirit without hearing an audible voice? Or was this just an inner prompting of the Holy Spirit? We don't know the answer. All we know is that the

Spirit directed Philip to go and speak to the Ethiopian in the chariot.

LET'S PRAY NOW

Can Christians rely on the inner prompting of the Holy Spirit to guide them today? The answer is probably, "Yes." God can lead His people intuitively: (1) If they are committed to doing God's will, (2) If they pray and seek God's direction, and (3) If they are spiritually in tune with the Holy Spirit.

However, let's make sure that we know there are dangers in seeking this type of direction from God. Remember, God speaks through His Word, and Christians can find the will of God in the Word of God. Also, remember we have an old nature and our flesh can tell us what it wants us to know and do: *"The sinful nature wants to do evil, which is just the opposite of what the Spirit wants. And the Spirit gives us desires that are the opposite of what the sinful nature desires. These two forces are constantly fighting each other, so you are not free to carry out your good intentions"* (Gal. 5:17 TLB). This verse tells us that our old nature is lurking within our mind to direct us away from God at the same time when we are praying for God to lead us into His will.

So what does this mean? Not every internal inclination that you have is from God. Again, the answer is in the Word of God. If you know Scripture and are abiding in Scripture, and you're letting the Word of God guide your life, then probably the Holy Spirit can lead you through *intuitive direction.*

15

Mountain–Moving Answers

When We Use Our Faith Supernaturally to Move God's Work Forward

EVERYONE KNOWS THE FAITH CHALLENGE to move mountains, *"For assuredly, I say to you, whoever says to this mountain, 'Be removed and be cast into the sea,' and does not doubt in his heart, but believes that those things he says will be done, he will have whatever he says. Therefore I say to you, whatever things you ask when you pray, believe that you receive them, and you will have them"* (Mark 11:23-24).

Jerry Falwell's boyhood home was located on the east end of the mountain that is today called Liberty. As a young boy, Jerry had walked every path on that mountain while hunting squirrels and rabbits. After he had planted Thomas Road Baptist Church (1957) and after he had begun Liberty University (1971), he decided to walk across every part of that mountain called Candler's Mountain in his boyhood—claiming it as a place for a great Christian training center that would reach the world.

In the mid '70s Jerry was flying into Lynchburg when he looked down on Liberty Mountain, the site of his boyhood dreams. He casually said to the real estate agent sitting behind him, "Who owns that property?"

The agent replied, "U.S. Gypsum."

Jerry asked, "Is it for sale?"

The agent responded, "*Everything* is for sale."

It was then that Jerry walked the mountain, claiming every foot of the 4,000 acres for God.

Jerry knew God's challenge to Joshua, "*Every place that the sole of your foot will tread upon I have given you...*" (Josh. 1:3). This promise was a repetition of what God told Abraham, "*And the Lord said to Abram, after Lot had separated from him: 'Lift your eyes now and look from the place where you are—northward, southward, eastward, and westward; for all the land which you see I give to you and your descendants forever'*" (Gen. 13:14-15). Based on what God showed Abraham, he said, "*Arise, walk in the land through its length and its width, for I give it to you*" (Gen. 13:17).

A little later, Jerry phoned the U.S. Gypsum headquarters to make an appointment to talk with the vice president in charge of real estate. Then Jerry and the same real estate agent who had flown with him when he first thought about buying the land walked into the Chicago office of U.S. Gypsum.

"How did you know the land was for sale?" the vice president asked Jerry.

Jerry did not know that at a recent board meeting, U.S. Gypsum had decided to sell off several real estate holdings across America to raise capital. They wanted $1,250,000 for the mountain in Lynchburg. Up to that time, the property had not been advertised, nor had anyone been told outside the organization that the mountain was for sale.

Jerry knew the power of vision; it's the way he motivated his church to action, and specifically to sacrifice. Jerry began telling the vice president his vision of building a great Christian university on the mountain. Jerry shared with him that God would take care of their every need, but inwardly the vice president was not so sure about God's bank account.

"Can I buy the property with a down payment and would U.S. Gypsum carry the mortgage for us?"

"Well, yes...," the vice president stammered.

At that moment, Jerry had no idea where the money was coming from except he knew that God was in the deal. He knew God wanted to have the land and knew that God would supply the money.

"We'll need $100,000 down payment," was the vice president's condition for setting up the mortgage. He snickered to himself, knowing that a $100,000 was too much for the small church.

"Would you take a $10,000 down payment and give me 30 days to raise $100,000?" Jerry asked the vice president. Jerry was asking them to accept a down payment on the down payment.

The real estate friend from Lynchburg knew that was the wrong thing to say. He shook his head "no" for Jerry to see, but not so the VP could see.

"Yes…" the vice president laughed to Jerry's request, not knowing what to make of this small town pastor with audacious faith.

Jerry knew that his army of Door Keepers was growing. These were people who gave him a $1 a week to support the new University and television ministry. Jerry had gone throughout Central Virginia and North Carolina in local churches asking people to give a $1 a week. He gave them 52 business reply envelopes stapled together; all they had to do was to slip a one dollar bill in the envelope and mail it to Lynchburg to become part of reaching the world for Christ.

Many Door Keepers will give me $100 for this property, Jerry thought to himself.

A secretary for U.S. Gypsum typed a letter of agreement and Jerry handed the $10,000 check over to the vice president who was still not sure why he was completing the deal.

As they walked out of the office Jerry turned and asked, "Could you hold that $10,000 check for about a week? I've got to raise enough money to cover it!"

At this point, the vice president really began to laugh out loud.

Jerry Falwell believed in *faith vision*; if God has put a vision in your heart of what He wants to do, God will supply those needs.

"And my God shall supply all your need according to His riches in glory by Christ Jesus" (Phil. 4:19).

Within a few days Jerry was able to cover the check for $10,000, and within 30 days Jerry had raised $100,000 for the down payment on the loan. But that great answer to prayer is not as great as what would happen 30 years later.

The Biggest Summer Ever

In the summer of 2004 everything on Liberty Mountain seemed to come together...everything. God blessed exceedingly abundantly above all that the prayer warriors at Thomas Road Baptist Church could think or ask (see Eph. 3:20). Next to Liberty University was the Ericsson factory of 880,000 square feet on 113 acres. Its replacement value was more than $100 million. Ericsson manufactured cell phones in this building, but these jobs went to China. The major Swedish conglomerate made a corporate decision to sell all its American properties. Immediately Jerry Falwell placed a bid of $2,000,000, but Ericsson rejected that bid as too low.

When Ericsson received no other offers for the property, they came back and asked Jerry Falwell to re-submit a bid. He said he would not do it unless there was an absolute auction, meaning that the lowest price would get the property. They agreed and set a minimum of $10 million. Then Jerry Falwell submitted a bid of over $10,200,000; still there were no other bidders.

Ericsson's attorneys advised Jerry Falwell Jr., the in-house attorney for Liberty University at the time, that they wanted to close the deal on February 14—Valentine's Day 2003. This meant that Jerry needed to raise $10,200,000 before that day. There was simply too little time to raise that amount of money, so the bankers agreed to come up with whatever additional amount was needed by February 14 so Liberty could buy this property.

February 14 came, but the lawyers for Ericsson were wrapped up in another deal in another city, so they faxed legal papers for the continuation of the sale for seven days.

That same day, Jerry Falwell flew to Oklahoma City to meet with Mr. David Green and his family, owner of Hobby Lobby, a chain of about 300 craft stores nationwide. David Green is a Christian philanthropist and committed to spreading the gospel of Jesus Christ worldwide.

Several months earlier, Hobby Lobby had offered to donate a major piece of property in the Greater Chicago area to Liberty University as a branch University campus. The Chicago property was located in a brand-new 300,000 square foot building on 80 acres, but Liberty turned it down because it didn't fit into their long-range plans. Liberty wanted to consolidate on its Lynchburg campus and not diversify around the United States. So Falwell flew to Oklahoma City to politely decline the Hobby Lobby gift offer. In Jerry's first three-hour meeting with David Green, he told him about the Ericsson facility in Lynchburg that he was buying.

David Green said Hobby Lobby would purchase the Ericsson property and donate it to the ministry. Attorneys for Hobby Lobby and Jerry Falwell Jr. had only five days and nights of telephone, e-mail discussions, and legal activity to close the sale on the Ericsson property—February 19. The gigantic Ericsson facilities miraculously and immediately became available to Liberty, debt free.

In the first year Liberty leased the building for $1 from Hobby Lobby and the following year the building was donated to Liberty.

Falwell said, "I find myself almost stunned at what a glorious and sudden thing our Lord had done for us. We are over ten million dollars ahead of where we thought we would be."

Liberty entered the Ericsson building debt free. The money that was planned to purchase the Ericsson property was then available to the university to convert and renovate the facilities for the use of Liberty University.

The following summer in 2004 everything on Liberty Mountain came together in abundance: new buildings, paved roads, sports facilities, and much more.

In 2004 Liberty added 2,943 new students, pushing the total enrollment to 8,453, the largest enrollment in history.

During that summer Liberty completed 19 new four-story dormitories at $1 million each, holding a combined total of roughly 1,600 more students than the university could sleep in previous years.

These dorms were located on the east side of the expressway, so a $1 million tunnel was dug under the expressway so the students could walk safely to class.

Also that year, the university built recreational facilities, a dining clubhouse, and an outside swimming pool near the new dormitories. They also built within the Ericsson facilities five basketball courts, weight rooms, a cafeteria, and a new NCAA regulation-sized swimming pool for sports competition, and dozens of classrooms.

Since faith moves mountains, Liberty moved dirt off an unusable hill to construct a 1,000-space parking lot and fill in an unusable 60-foot deep ravine next to the football field which became a second 1,000-space parking lot.

During that summer Liberty received a $4.5 million gift for a football operations center, a new two-story building at the north end of the football field with Jeffersonian columns through which people enter.

Also, as Liberty moved into the Ericsson facilities, it began a new Liberty University School of Law, costing over $5 million in renovations, and a $5 million legal library.

A gift was given for a new $5 million ice hockey complex, and that year Liberty was ranked number seven among the NCAA Division I colleges.

And then, when everything else seemed overwhelming, Thomas Road Baptist Church signed a contract with Kodiak Construction to begin a 6,500-seat sanctuary on the new campus that would cost $20 million. Ericsson already had 5,000 parking spaces, but 2,000 more were added, costing another $200,000.

Also, a $7 million contract was signed with Kodiak to refurbish the north end of Ericsson into classrooms for Sunday school, and Liberty Christian Academy, a K through grade 12 Christian school with over 1,000 students. And while all of this seems overwhelming, it was done without borrowing any additional monies. During 2004 Liberty received over $55 million in gifts from many different sources, all because of answers to prayers.

Sunday school enrollment jumped from 4,000 to over 8,000 a year later. Church attendance jumped from 5,000 to over 12,000 the same year. And within the next two years, Liberty jumped from nearly 5,000 students on campus to an enrollment of over 10,000 students.

LET'S PRAY NOW

When praying for big things, make sure your emphasis is never on big things. Think in terms of *faith priority*. For God to answer great prayers or to give you great rewards, you must make sure your priorities fit into God's priorities. God is not interested in buildings for the sake of buildings, nor does God get a lot of glory out of owning large acreages of land.

First, God's priority is reaching people and/or teaching people. So begin with people, then trust God to supply buildings, programs, and money to reach people for Christ and teach them the Word of God. Too often churches fail because their whole emphasis is on buildings, or land, or "stuff." Many churches suffer because they've never learned the *faith priority* of people ministry.

Second, you must learn to excel in what you are doing for God, rather than placing emphasis on doing more for God. If a ministry will do an outstanding job of ministry, it will attract other people because of its excellent ministry, whether that would be evangelism, discipleship, or counseling. Whatever you do, do it excellently all to the glory of God (see Col. 3:23).

Third, there must be spiritual integrity if you want to have the full blessing of God on your work. When the Word of God works in the lives of His people, then that's the best basis for any big bold prayers you will make.

Just signing a doctrinal statement that you believe the Word of God and the fundamentals of the faith is not enough. God is not impressed with autographs, but if you believe the Bible is the Word of God, then give it your attention in study and preaching, but most of all, in your life. When God sees your integrity, He has a basis for answering with awesome results.

Fourth, remember God honors simple childlike faith. Faith is simply taking God at His Word, and believing what He has said. So you must plan your life and ministry around the principles of the Word of God.

The aim of a church is not to be smarter than the world, stronger than the world, surely not richer than the world. The church must center on faith to believe what God has said, then go out and do it. When the church exercises faith and obedience, it will have all the wisdom it needs, all the strength it needs, and all the money it needs because the Bible has promised, *"And my God shall supply all your need according to His riches in glory..."* (Phil. 4:19).

16

Prayer Warfare Answers

*When You Pray Defensively Against Evil That Is
Attacking You, or You Pray Aggressively Against Evil
That Is Oppressing You or the Work of God*

P RAYER WARFARE INVOLVES TWO STRATEGIES: first, praying
defensively when you are attacked by the evil one and second, praying offensively when you seek to deliver a ministry and/or individual from domination or attacks from the evil one.

DEFENSIVE SPIRITUAL WARFARE

Two times in my life I have felt *atmospheric evil*; this is when you feel the presence of evil around you. This is opposite from the experience of *atmospheric presence* of God. God describes revival as, *"I will pour out My spirit upon all flesh"* (Joel 2:28, Acts 2:18). And what does God do when He pours out revival? He pours Himself into a revival meeting, or a situation that needs renewal and reviving. This is God's atmospheric presence.

The *atmospheric presence* of God can also be felt in worship because Jesus said, *"the Father is seeking such to worship Him"* (John 4:23). So, when a believer truly worships God from the heart, God will come to receive that worship, bringing His presence into that worship experience.

On New Year's Eve 1977 I was in Haiti, a nation that probably has more witchcraft, demon-possession, and spirit worship than any other nation in the world. There were approximately 40 Liberty University students with me and they were living in a camp dormitory that had belonged to the Haiti Baptist Mission.

I had gone to bed early that evening, sleeping on the back screened porch of missionaries Wallace and Eleanor Turnbull's home. At midnight I was awakened by the blaring of ships' horns in the harbor, as well as the chiming of steeple bells. If ever there was a time and place that satan manifested himself, this was it.

Suddenly I felt a lurking evil presence on the back porch with me. I didn't see anything, I didn't wrestle with anything, nor did I physically touch anything. It was a frightening internal sense.

"Evil is here," I said to myself, then shuddered in fear.

I know there are three things that repel evil: (1) the name of Jesus, (2) the blood of Jesus, and (3) the Cross. So I began to sing songs about the blood of Jesus,

"What can wash away my sin?
Nothing but the blood of Jesus.
What can make me whole again?
Nothing but the blood of Jesus.
Oh! precious is the flow
That makes me white as snow;
No other fount I know,
Nothing but the blood of Jesus."[1]

I got tremendous confidence singing about the blood of Jesus Christ, and it focused me on Jesus, away from any evil that was present. Then I began to ask myself, "What's another song about the blood of Jesus?"

"There is a fountain filled with blood
Drawn from Emmanuel's veins;
And sinners plunged beneath that flood
Lose all their guilty stains.
Lose all their guilty stains,

Lose all their guilty stains;
And sinners plunged beneath that flood
Lose all their guilty stains."[2]

I sang for a long time, forgetting where I was and my immediate problem. In my mind I went back to the Cross where Jesus died for me; in my heart I worshiped the Lord. Then I began to sing again,

"When I survey the wondrous cross
On which the Prince of glory died,
My richest gain I count but loss,
And pour contempt on all my pride."

Forbid it, Lord, that I should boast,
Save in the death of Christ my God!
All the vain things that charm me most,
I sacrifice them to His blood."[3]

There was another time when I felt the presence of evil. In 1974 I was swimming in the Moon River (yes, it's the river that Johnny Mercer wrote about in the famous song in the movies, *Breakfast at Tiffany's*. My father and Johnny Mercer had been good friends and my father had helped Johnny with a project on Moon River).

I was half swimming and half floating in the high tide, when suddenly I felt the presence of evil. Because I was sensitive to the Holy Spirit, I began to sing again a song about the blood of Jesus. Of course, I prayed,

"Lord…whatever evil is here…protect me from it."

I slowly swam back to the dock, climbed out, and shivered all over—not from cold, but fear. Standing there, I prayed,

"Lord, I don't know what you saved me from, but I'd rather follow your inclination and be safe; rather than ignore Your leading and be sorry."

LET'S PRAY NOW

The following is a description of spiritual warfare when dealing with demons. First, casting out demons is not something the exorcist does by his power—it is in the power of God. He must begin by recognizing the blood of Jesus Christ that cleanses from sin and the power of the Cross of Christ are the only basis for helping anyone spiritually. The exorcist must be sure he or she has confessed all sin and is in fellowship with Christ.

Second, there must be a choice by the demonized person that he or she wants to be rid of the demon.

Third, during the exorcism there must be an exposure of the demon as a demon. Most demon possession is hidden and observers do not perceive the person as demonized.

In the fourth place, the person has to decide whether he or she is going to follow God and be free of the demon, or if the person is going to yield to the demon and remain in a possessed state. Just as God does not heal those who do not want to be healed, God will not cast out the demon for those who do not want the demon cast out.

Fifth, the role of the exorcist is to share faith, strength, and wisdom with the person who needs help. The role of the exorcist is to witness what God can do in building up the faith of the person who is demon possessed. Then the demonized person can make a decision to be free.

Sixth, ultimate exorcism is not in the power of the person who is helping, nor is it in the power of the patient; but in the power of God who wrestles directly with satan. The demon is cast out by the blood of Jesus Christ.

Seventh, it is by faith that a person is free from the demon.[4]

ENDNOTES

1. Robert Lowry, *Nothing but the Blood of Jesus*, http://www.subversiveinfluence.com/wordpress/?p=1433, accessed 11 December 2008.

2. William Cowper, *There is a Fountain Filled with Blood*, http://www.cyberhymnal.org/htm/t/f/tfountfb.htm, accessed 11 December 2008.

3. Isaac Watts, *When I Survey the Wondrous Cross*, http://www.cyberhymnal.org/htm/w/h/e/whenisur.htm, accessed 11 December 2008.

4. Taken from Elmer Towns' book, *Theology for Today*, Harcourt and Brace (Dallas, TX, 2002). For more help see Doris Wagner, *How to Cast Out Demons: A Beginner's Guide* (Ventura, CA: Regal Books, 1999).

SECTION

THE WAY GOD GIVES
ANSWERS

Sometimes God does really big things for us just to let us know that He is a God who can do really big things. But if He did that all the time, our faith would be based on the really big things, and not based on God Himself.

Ingersoll, the great atheist, stood before an audience over 200 years ago, took out his pocket watch, and defied God,

"God—if you're there—I defy you to strike me dead within one minute."

Ingersoll counted off the seconds, and when he didn't die, he pronounced, "There you have it, there is no God."

An unknown pastor approached him and said, "God is like a stationmaster who dispenses His great roaring trains on a set schedule. God doesn't change His schedule just to smash a 'worm' on the tracks."

This section suggests the many times on God's schedule when He hears our prayers and dispatches His "great roaring trains" for our benefit.

17

Barrier Answers

Instead of Answering Our Prayers, God Allows an
Obstacle to Tell Us "No, It Will Not Happen"

MY GOOD FRIENDS Art and Marilyn Winn planned to go as missionaries to New Guinea. Even though they felt called of God, they didn't make it. They even went through Wycliffe linguistics school to learn how to be Bible translators, but they didn't make it to the mission field. Their 2½-year-old son was diagnosed with celiac disease and could not eat any grains (wheat, rye, oats, barley, etc.). It is a lifelong ailment, so they couldn't get to jungle-training camp; they resigned their position from the mission board. To Art this was God's closed door to the mission field.

There may be other things for which you pray, and suddenly a barrier drops in front of you. Now not every barrier is an absolute "no." Perhaps a church wants to build a new sanctuary, but every bank they approach for a loan turns them down. Is this God's "no"? Does God want them to wait to build, or does God want them to get money from some other source?

Sometimes a young person prays about entering college, but his GPA is too low, or he doesn't meet other qualifications, so he's turned down. Is this a *barrier answer*? Should he go to a community college to raise his grades, or should he attend a technical school to learn a trade? What is God saying through "no"?

Sometimes a barrier is not really a barrier; it is God's obstacle course. God wants to test our integrity to see if we are sincere in obeying Him. Or God wants to test us to see if we have faith to say to the mountain, "Remove!"

What's the difference between a barrier and an obstacle course? A barrier is when the door is closed, and there is no way to go forward. God speaks to us through closed doors, as well as through open doors. He is the God of the "doors" in our life.

Sometimes an obstacle course tests our patience; perhaps we need to learn endurance before praying again. Sometimes God wants to test our faith—to make our faith stronger—so the challenge is to pray again and again. Isn't that what Jesus meant when He said, *"Ask* [the Greek says 'keep on asking'] *and it will be given to you"* (Matt. 7:7)?

One of the more famous *barrier answers* is found at Kadesh Barnea in the wilderness (Num. 13:1–14:45). God's people had come out of Egyptian slavery and sat for approximately one year at the foot of Mount Sinai where God organized them into a self-existing nation. The nation then left Sinai and came to Kadesh Barnea.

The nation sent out twelve reconnaissance spies to determine what the land of promise looked like. Ten spies brought back negative reports of great enemies, tall-walled cities, and impossible obstacles. Two spies brought back a positive report that God could conquer their enemies and they could possess the land.

Not only did Israel say "no" to entering the Promised Land, they said, *"Let us make a captain, and let us return to Egypt"* (Num. 14:4). In spite of Moses' pleading with them, Israel refused to enter the Promised Land.

God told them that they would wander in the wilderness for 40 years until everyone 20 years old and above died there, *"They certainly shall not see the land of which I swore to their fathers"* (Num. 14:23). God went on to say in the same verse, *"nor shall any of those who rejected me see it."* What good thing did God promise? *"Your little ones…I will bring in, and they shall know the land that you have despised"* (Num. 14:31).

What was the result of God's judgment on them? The people in essence said, "I'm sorry." They are like a lot of children today who say "I'm sorry," but they don't mean, "I'll never do it again." They mean, "I'm sorry I got caught." What about Israel? *"The people mourned greatly"* (Num. 14:39).

The next day they repented and said, *"we will go up to the place which the Lord has promised"* (Num. 14:40). They prayed for God to change His mind and allow them to go into the Promised Land. The people started to go in spite of God's "no." God didn't go with them, *"They presume to go up, nevertheless the Shekinah glory cloud departed not out of the camp"* (Num. 14:44 ELT).

Because they had sinned against God and wouldn't trust His leadership, God said "no" and that generation never entered the Promised Land.

You may have said "no" to God in the past, and maybe you can never do in the future what you refused to do in the past. Remember, God will forgive your sin and have fellowship with you…but maybe the *barrier answer* remains standing.

LET'S PRAY NOW

When God says "no" we must learn to yield to His answer and do His will. In the case of my friends Art and Marilyn Winn, they became lifelong faithful workers in their local church. They had a passion to serve God: she was a nurse in a local hospital, and Art spent his life as a director of human resources in a Presbyterian home for children.

Some of God's people have gone through divorce, and there are many churches that will not ordain a divorced minister, nor will they hire one. If you have had a divorce, even if you were the innocent party, what are you to do in the face of closed doors? My answer is simple; don't go through life banging on closed doors. There are denominations and local churches that will ordain and/or accept a divorced person. Also, there are other places in ministry where you can serve without ordination. Don't spend your life banging on closed doors; go looking for open doors.

Life is too short and there are too many places that need people to serve God. Find a harvest field where there are no workers, and go serve the Lord today.

18

Blind Answers

*When You Pray for an Answer, You Know God Can
Do Something, and That He Will Answer; but You
Don't Know How God Will Answer*

MARTHA WAS THE CONSCIENTIOUS HOUSEKEEPER who seemed to be always cooking meals, setting tables, and looking after the details. Her brother Lazarus grew desperately ill. Martha and her sister Mary sent word to Jesus that Lazarus was sick (John 11:2).

Jesus waited four days before going to Bethany. Jesus waited just long enough for Lazarus to die. When Jesus got there, Martha—the control freak—could hardly contain her irritation. She said to Jesus, *"Lord, if You had been here, my brother would not have died"* (John 11:21). Perfectionists never blame themselves, and they certainly don't allow circumstances to disrupt their lives.

But now Martha was desperate. Her brother was dead, and the future seemed bleak. So Martha blindly searched for an answer. She wanted Jesus to do something, but she was not sure what she wanted:

"But even now I know that whatever You ask of God, God will give You" (John 11:22).

Praying blindly is asking God to do something, when you don't know what should be done. Because you're frustrated, hopeless, or completely boxed up in a dead-end canyon; you are praying for a *blind answer*, "Thy will be done." You pray for God to do something but you don't know what, or how God will answer.

Why do you pray blindly? Because you've tried to do everything possible. Wasn't that true about Martha? She was the model house-keeper who had everything under control; everything, that is, but death. She even called for Jesus to come and heal her brother; she tried to control her brother's sickness by calling on Jesus. But Jesus didn't come when she wanted and her brother died. Now there was nothing else she could do. Death ends it all; it's God's final statement to every perfectionist. They can't control the day of death.

Martha prayed for a *blind answer, "But even now I know that whatever You ask of God, God will give You"* (John 11:22).

Esther prayed blindly when she faced her possible death and a possible holocaust of the entire Jewish nation. Everyone knows the story that Haman the prime minister hated Jews and had arranged for the king to sign a decree that anyone who killed a Jew could keep their property and estate. From the human point of view, it seemed that nothing could be done to save the entire nation, because the law of the Medes and Persians declared no law could be changed.

Esther was willing to go into the presence of the king, even if it meant her death. She was seeking a *blind answer* when she told her uncle Mordecai, *"Go, gather all the Jews who are present in Shushan, and fast for me; neither eat nor drink for three days, night or day. My maids and I will fast likewise. And so I will go to the king, which is against the law; and if I perish, I perish!"* (Esther 4:16).

When the three Hebrew young men were about to be cast into the burning furnace because they refused to bow to the idol of Nebuchadnezzar, they manifested the same blind faith as Esther (Dan. 3:3-25). The three young men told Nebuchadnezzar, *"Our God whom we serve is able to deliver us from the burning fiery furnace.... But if not..."* (Dan. 3:17-18). When the young men said, "But if not," they realized God may not deliver them. They realized they may die. What then? If God didn't deliver, their future was unknown. Blind faith?

The three young men had the key to blindness—they surrendered to God. They put their trust in God to deliver them, *"but if not."* They were willing to die because they declared, *"We do not serve your gods, nor will we worship the gold image which you have set up"* (Dan. 3:18). *Blind answers* are waiting for the consequences that are unknown.

LET'S PRAY NOW

When you pray blindly, you don't know what God will do, but you know that God must do something. The prayer for *blind answers* assumes that: (1) you have faith that God will do something, (2) you are yielded for whatever answer God sends, and (3) you'll accept the consequences if God doesn't answer. Wasn't this Esther's acquiescence, *"If I perish, I perish"*? Wasn't that the answer of the three young men, *"But if not…"*?

Blind answers lead to all types of responses in the human who prays to God. Sometimes we are thrilled with an answer we didn't expect. So we bow in worship to thank God.

Sometimes we get a hard answer. We lose money, or lose possession, or we lose our place in life as we line up to get ahead. Sometimes we're punished, and even at times, some are martyred. When "loss" happens, we can either complain, or submit passively, or renounce God, or we can praise God as did Job, *"The Lord gave, and the Lord has taken away; blessed be the name of the Lord"* (Job 1:21).

19

Circumstantial Answers

When God Works Through Circumstances
to Give Us the Answers We Desire

SOMETIMES WHEN YOU PRAY, GOD does not answer your prayer the way you expect; rather, God rearranges circumstances to answer your prayer. Remember, Esther was married to King Xerxes when Prime Minister Haman, who hated the Jews, arranged for a law to be enacted that gave anyone the right to kill a Jew and keep their money or property.

When Esther learned of the imminent holocaust, she knew she had to appeal to the king, but she didn't have access to the king. If she entered unannounced, there could be dire consequences unless the king held out his scepter when she entered his throne room.

Esther asked the Jews, *"Fast for me....I also, and my maidens will fast likewise"* (Esther 4:16). Esther committed her life or death on a *circumstantial answer* to her prayer, *"If I perish, I perish"* (Esther 4:16).

Notice what God didn't do: He didn't change the obscene law, He didn't make the king call Esther, He didn't eliminate Haman, and God didn't solve the problem directly. God answered the prayer by working supernaturally—behind the scenes—through circumstances.

First, Esther planned a feast to get the king in a good mood for her request. Then God allowed Haman's anger to become so white hot that he planned to hang Mordecai, Esther's uncle. Next, God used the king's sleeplessness so that someone read to him "dusty" official records where he learned Mordecai had saved him. The next morning King Xerxes had Haman honor "Mordecai, the Jew." At the banquet that night, Easter revealed her Jewish identity and that Haman was trying to kill all Jews. When the king went out of the room "to cool off," Haman grabbed Esther by the legs. When the king returned he thought Haman was trying to have sex with his wife. He had Haman hanged on the gallows prepared for Mordecai. God worked through circumstances to answer prayer.

Let's Pray Now

Sometimes God doesn't answer our prayers directly, but He works indirectly. It's easy for God to do a miracle. He, who has power over His laws, can easily adjust His laws to do His will. But sometimes God doesn't answer our prayers with a miracle. He works behind the scenes to give us what we ask.

Sometimes it takes more effort by God to coordinate many details to bring about an answer than it would if God would just snap His miraculous fingers to get a job done. But if God were in the "finger-snapping business," then people would probably pray for the wrong reason, and serve God for the wrong reason.

There are many different ways that God answers prayers—almost 50 written in this book. God answers according to our need to grow, or according to the need of ministry, or according to the workings of His nature. Sometimes, God answers according to the needs of others.

But maybe God likes to work through circumstances—behind the scenes so people won't follow Him for the wrong reason. If every time we asked for something in prayer and God snapped His fingers, people would think that God ran errands for His followers. They would follow God to get things done, not because they loved God with all their hearts (see Matt. 22:36-38), or because Christ died for them, or for any of the other biblical motives. No, they would follow God because He did things for them.

But, *all things work together for good to those who love God* (Rom. 8:28).

20

Delayed Answers

When God Waits a Period of Time Before Answering Our Requests

WHEN SIN RUNS RAMPANT AND no one seems to be obeying God, then God's servant must do something spectacular to call people back to God. That's what Elijah did because, *"Ahab did more to provoke the Lord God of Israel to anger than all the kings of Israel who were before him"* (1 Kings 16:33). To point out the nation's sin, *"Elijah…said to Ahab, 'As the Lord God of Israel lives, before whom I stand, there shall not be dew nor rain these years, except at my word'"* (1 Kings 17:1).

The New Testament describes Elijah as one who "prayed earnestly." Here prayer is an unusual Greek word, *proseuchomai*, which appears twice. This is like saying, "He prayed a prayer," so this Hebraic expression suggests intensity. Elijah prayed with all of his heart that it would not rain for three and a half years.

Now let's look at the conclusion of three and a half years. Elijah again prayed this time for the heavens to give rain. *"Then Elijah said to Ahab, "Go up, eat and drink; for there is the sound of abundance of rain.".…And Elijah went up to the top of Carmel; then he bowed down on the ground, and put his face between his knees, and said to his servant, "Go up now, look toward the sea." So he went up and looked, and said, "There is nothing." And seven times he said, "Go again." Then it came to pass the seventh time, that he said, "There is a cloud, as small as a man's hand, rising out of the sea!" So he said, "Go up, say to Ahab, 'Prepare your chariot, and go down before the rain stops you'"* (1 Kings 18:41-44). After Elijah prayed seven times, finally a torrential storm broke over the land.

God didn't answer the first time Elijah prayed. God heard the request of Elijah. But God waited while Elijah kept praying. God probably waited for a storm front to form (it takes time for weather conditions to evolve). Within time, God answers. Maybe the same thing happens in our lives. God hears our request, but it takes time for God to work through circumstances to deliver His answer to us.

As mentioned previously, when I first went to Columbia Bible College, I was assigned to Legsters Hall that was filled with WWII veterans. Many of these older men had been called to pastor small country churches where they preached on the weekend, which supplied them money to go through college. I found myself in many prayer meetings praying with these older men, where I begged, "God give me a church…God give me a church."

God probably laughed as He looked down from Heaven into my immature heart. I was not ready to pastor a church; I was only willing and eager to do it. If I had listened carefully to the whisper of God, I might have heard God say, "Wait."

God delayed answering my request because I was too young and immature. Sometimes God delays because we are not ready for Him to answer. In the next year and a half I learned many lessons. I preached my first sermon at a street meeting, taught a Sunday school class each week at a Presbyterian mission, and learned to lead souls to Christ.

In September of my second year of college God saw that I was ready to pastor a church, even though I was only 19 years old. Mrs. Silla Hair came to a Youth for Christ rally where I was leading singing. Afterward she asked, "Will you be our pastor?"

The Westminster Presbyterian Church in inner city Savannah had been decommissioned and closed because all the rich people of the neighborhood had moved away to better neighborhoods. When the poor moved in, Mrs. Hair got a key to the building, and with five ladies she opened it to begin a Sunday school for about 15 children. That was the first church I pastored (see *Stories About My First Church* at www.elmertowns.com.

There are many other reasons why God delays His answer. Sometimes we are not spiritually ready, as I was not spiritually or physically ready to be a pastor. At other times God must prepare circumstances before our requests can be answered. Sometimes God lets us continue praying to test our faith or sincerity. Doesn't the Scripture say, *"Therefore the Lord will wait, that He may be gracious to you"* (Isa. 30:18)?

Sometimes you ask God to do something but He doesn't say "yes" or "no"! He doesn't seem to say anything—at least you think He ignores you—but God answers after a period of time.

LET'S PRAY NOW

If God has not answered your prayer, first check your spiritual life. Is there any sin blocking your intercession? Do you have faith to believe God will answer this prayer? Have you prayed with all your heart? If your answer is "yes," then keep on praying. God may be delaying the answer.

There's a second area of concern. Check the thing for which you are praying. Is your request biblical? Does it fit within God's priority for doing ministry? Look ahead at Section IV, The "No" Answers to Our Prayers. God may have a reason He is not answering. Are you sure the request is what God wants done?

The third area deals with spiritual reasons why God is silent. Maybe God wants you to grow more spiritually before He answers. Maybe God hasn't answered because He's waiting to see your sincerity, or He is waiting for events to unfold before He answers. There are many good reasons why God waits to answer our prayers.

The Bible teaches us to wait on God. *"Let no one who waits on You be ashamed"* (Ps. 25:3). *"Wait on the Lord; be of good courage, and He shall strengthen your heart; wait, I say, on the Lord!"* (Ps. 27:14).

21

Directional Answers

When God Answers by Directing Us What to Do

SOMETIMES GOD DOESN'T ANSWER YOUR prayer to give you the thing you request. Rather, He tells you where to get the thing for which you pray. God gives you a task or direction how to answer the prayer yourself.

Hagar was the maidservant of Abraham who delivered a son to him, Ishmael. Later, Sarah, the wife of Abraham, had a son, Isaac. The older son Ishmael fought with the young son, Isaac, and Sarah said to her husband, *"Cast out this bondwoman and her son"* (Gen. 21:10).

Abraham sent her away with a bottle of water and bread.

As Hagar and her son Ishmael crossed the desert going back toward her home in Egypt, they got lost in the hot sun and were about to die. Hagar said, *"Let me not see the death of the boy. So she sat opposite him, and lifted her voice and wept"* (Gen. 21:16).

Then God spoke to her from Heaven, *"Fear not, for God has heard the voice of the lad"* (Gen. 21:17). God showed her the location of a well of water. *"Then God opened her eyes, and she saw a well of water. And she went and filled the skin with water, and gave the lad a drink"* (Gen. 21:19).

Sometimes when you pray for things like food or water, God doesn't give them to you miraculously; rather, God shows you where you can find them. Maybe God doesn't give you food to eat, nor does He send money; God gives you a job to make money. Maybe God doesn't heal you, but He directs you to a doctor, or to medicine that will bring about healing.

Remember, Elijah had prayed for it not to rain upon the earth and it didn't for three and a half years (James 5:17-18). As a result of the famine, there was no food anywhere. Even King Ahab was out scrounging for food.

The Bible doesn't say that Elijah prayed for food during this famine. *"The word of the Lord came to him* [Elijah], *saying, 'Get away from here and turn eastward, and hide by the Brook Cherith...'"* (1 Kings 17:2-3). There the ravens providentially brought food to him, morning and evening, and he drank from the brook. But when the brook dried up, God sent him into Zarephath (modern-day Lebanon). This time God didn't provide his food providentially, rather he gave him an advice answer or a *directional answer.* God said, *"Arise, go to Zarephath, which belongs to Sidon, and dwell there. See, I have commanded a widow there to provide for you"* (1 Kings 17:9).

Have you ever been guilty of asking God to do something, only to find out later God wants *you* to do something to answer your prayer?

Sometimes we're lost and we ask God to help us get where we're going. God doesn't work a supernatural miracle to guide us there; He leads us to a convenience store where we can get directions.

When a frustrated and discouraged farmer prayed for God to grow a crop of soybeans on his ground, he expected that next year the seed he planted would produce soybeans. But God didn't do the miraculous answer the farmer expected; rather, the county agent that was paid by the government to help farmers came by and told the farmer he was planting the soybeans too deeply and they were rotting in the ground. Also, the county agent told him his ground needed lime to grow a great crop of soybeans. After following the county agent's advice, the next year was an abundant "bumper" crop. God answered his prayers by giving him advice and direction.

On the road to Damascus, Paul saw the Lord and was converted. Perhaps the pure shining light of Jesus Christ blinded Paul. It was then that Paul yielded to Christ and prayed, *"Lord, what do You want me to do?"* (Acts 9:6).

At the time, Jesus did not miraculously cure his eyes to help him see. Rather, Jesus gave him a *directional answer.* *"Arise and go into the city, and you will be told what you must do"* (Acts 9:6).

When Paul arrived in the city, *"he was three days without sight, and neither ate nor drank"* (Acts 9:9). Can you imagine the agony and fear that raced through his mind? Paul probably thought he would be blind for life. Do you think he prayed for healing?

God was going to do a miracle and give Paul back his eyesight, but at first, the Lord only gave him a *directional answer.* If Paul had not obeyed God's instructions, would God have not healed him? That's a pointless question because Paul *did* obey, and God *did* heal him.

Imbedded in that story is a second *advice answer* given by God. The Lord spoke to Ananias in a vision, *"Arise and go to the street called Straight, and inquire at the house of Judas for one called Saul of Tarsus, for behold, he is praying"* (Acts 9:11).

Ananias at first didn't want to obey because he heard rumors that Saul had come to Damascus to arrest and take Christians back to Jerusalem. *"But the Lord said to him, 'Go, for he is a chosen vessel of Mine to bear My name before Gentiles, kings, and the children of Israel'"* (Acts 9:15). So Ananias received the *directional answer,* and did what God told him to do. Ananias said to Paul, *"Brother Saul, receive your sight"* (Acts 22:13).

The very next chapter in Acts tells how God answered the prayers of Cornelius, a Roman army commander, with a *directional answer.* God told him, *"Now send men to Joppa, and send for Simon whose surname is Peter. …He will tell you what you must do"* (Acts 10:5-6). That sounds like God giving instructions how to get an answer to his prayers.

When the delegation from Cornelius reached Peter's house, Peter was praying on the roof. Because God wanted to send Peter to the Gentiles—considered unclean by the Jews—God gave Peter a vision of unclean animals. God let a sheet down from Heaven full of unclean animals, then told Peter, *"Rise, Peter; kill and eat"* (Acts 10:13). Peter saw the vision three times. Peter was not sure what it meant. Immediately, a delegation of Gentiles knocked on Peter's door. It was then when God told Peter, *"Arise therefore, go down and go with them, doubting nothing; for I have sent them"* (Acts 10:20). God gave a *directional answer* to the prayer of both Cornelius and Peter.

LET'S PRAY NOW

Be sensitive to the different ways that God might answer your prayers. When you pray for money, God might lead you to a job where you can earn a salary. When you pray for great results in Christian service, God might lead you to use a fellow worker who can accomplish what you can't do. When you pray for a turn of events in your family, God may show you what to do, and how you can get the results you seek.

Don't expect God to do something exactly the way you pray. God may want you to accomplish the results through your own initiative. However, this is not to say you shouldn't ask God to do anything, or everything. If you never pray, you may never get any answer. But when you pray, God may not give it to you; rather, He will lead you to an answer or direct you where the answer may be found.

22

Diversionary Answers

When God Answers Our Prayer Differently
From the Thing for Which We Ask

O NCE JONATHAN EDWARDS FASTED AND prayed for three days for God's outpouring on a sermon he prepared entitled "Sinner in the Hands of an Angry God." (It was an absolute fast because Edwards didn't eat or drink.) Two hours before he was to preach the sermon, Edwards began to gag and cough. He had to break his absolute fast to drink some water.

Edwards entered the pulpit a broken man because he violated his fast-vow to God. So rather than a powerful presentation, Edwards mounted the pulpit in humiliation. God changed his boldness to brokenness. But God anointed the sermon, not because of Edwards' bold preaching, but because of his brokenness.

That sermon began the First Great Awakening in the United States. In a *diversionary* or *different answer*, God doesn't answer using the method or thing for which he prayed. Rather, God may answer by using something else—something different—to answer our prayers.

There are several reasons why God uses *diversionary answers* than what we expect. Many times we are like the disciples when Jesus said of them, *"You do not know what you ask"* (Mark 10:38). We pray for God to send revival to our church through a particular evangelist who will preach deep spiritual sermons. But God doesn't answer the way we requested. God sends a different speaker who has His anointing for revival.

A pastor prayed for God to give him a son to carry on his legacy of ministry, but God gave him a girl baby. As she grew up, she became more committed to carrying on the influence of her father, more than anyone would have expected of her. She did it by testimony, by publishing his sermons, and by setting up a nonprofit foundation to carry on her father's legacy. And what did God do? God diverted the prayer of that pastor for a son, and answered it with a girl; and his daughter did what the pastor wanted done.

What about a businessman who prayed for the success of a product line so that his business would prosper financially, but the product line failed. Customers rejected the product en masse, but in the moment of abject failure, the businessman found a second product that his customers needed. God answered the businessman's prayer with financial success through a second product, but he would never have found it if the first product didn't fail.

Doesn't that remind us of God's dealing with Israel in the wilderness? The people prayed for a military victory over their enemies, but God didn't use the army of Israel, *"And I will send hornets before you, which shall drive out the Hivite, the Canaanite, and the Hittite from before you"* (Exod. 23:28).

An elderly man was having trouble with his memory, and daily he prayed, "Lord, help me remember." When that didn't work, he prayed "God, give me the ability to memorize as I had as a youth." Again that didn't work. God didn't answer the request as the man phrased it because the man was asking God to supernaturally intervene with his aging memory. It's as if God was saying, "No…that's not the way I do it." (See Chapter 42, No, That's Not the Way I Do It.)

The organization where he worked had been chosen by a German medical company for research for a new memory enhancement ginkgo drug.

In the sovereignty of God, the man was chosen to be a part of the test. The man didn't get the placebo, but the real thing. After taking ginkgo biloba for six weeks, the man showed the highest rate of memory growth of any person in the test group.

What could you say? God heard and answered the man's request, but not the way he wanted. The elderly man was asking God to do a miracle, but God used medical means, testing ginkgo biloba, to increase the man's memory. (See Chapter 24, Medical Answers.)

A Christian leader was having a sexual affair. A fellow worker had suspicions about the affair but could do nothing. He prayed for God to hide the affair so the work of God might not be tarnished.

God in Heaven laughed and splashed the news of the affair on the front page headlines, blared it from the six o'clock news, and every person in the metropolitan area knew about the affair. The holy God answered the prayer in a most unexpected way—He did the opposite of what was asked. The reputation of a Holy God is never tarnished when the heinous sins of one of His servants is publicized. The church is hurt and individual Christians become disillusioned, but God is God, and what God has said about His judgment of sin will always come true.

God has said, if you confess your sins publicly, "I will forgive them and separate them from you as far as the East is from the West, and remember them no more" (see Ps. 103:12). But if you hide your sin, God will bring them to light and tell the world what you've done wrong.

Paul wrote to the Romans that he was coming to see them, *"Whenever I journey to Spain, I shall come* [to Rome]...*to see you..."* (Rom. 15:24). Paul was so sure he would come to Rome that he invited the Romans to pray with him for deliverance from those attacking him so he could make the journey, *"that I may be delivered from those in Judea who do not believe, and that my service for Jerusalem may be acceptable to the saints"* (Rom. 15:31).

Did God answer Paul's prayer to be delivered from the Judaizers? No! Did Paul slip out of Jerusalem unnoticed and unharmed? No!

All the city of Jerusalem was in an uproar over his entrance. Paul was beaten by a mob and then was arrested.

Paul came to Rome in a much different way than he apparently expected. Paul came in chains with an armed guard. God answered his prayer, but God brought Paul to Rome in His own way. Paul was arrested by the Romans and given safe protection of Roman soldiers in a Roman jail. Paul lost his freedom, and spent the next four years in chains. (Two years in Caesarea and two years in Rome.)

Paul had prayed, *"That I may come to you* [in Rome] *with joy by the will of God, and may be refreshed together with you"* (Rom. 15:32). Paul did come to Rome by way of a long tedious voyage across the Mediterranean Sea where he faced storms, shipwreck, snake bites, and long periods without food. God answered Paul's prayer, but with a *diversionary answer.*

LET'S PRAY NOW

Learn the division of labor. We must do what only human beings can do, and let God do what only God will do. We must agonize in prayer, continually bringing the issue before God in prayer. Our commanded duty is to bring our requests before the Lord of the Universe, then stand back and watch God answer in His own unique way.

We must spend more time praising God for His results, rather than requesting the answers we seek and telling God how He must answer us.

Sometimes we pray much, but don't learn much, because our prayer is all about our needs and how we want things done. Our prayers are not about God and Who He is. When we learn the nature of God, we'll let Him answer our prayer the way He wishes.

When we spend much time in worship and adoration, we focus on God. The more we praise God for what He has done in the past, the more we learn about God; and we will learn what He can do in the future.

Also, we must spend more time worshiping God for what He has done in the past. When we do that, God is more likely to continue working for us today. In addition to that, worship puts us on "praying ground." Therefore, when we leave worship to enter our time of intercession, perhaps we are more likely to get our requests answered than previously when we only talked to God without listening to Him.

So don't tell God how to do His work; rather, ask God for His work to be accomplished and let God do it in His own way. God has always done it His way, but it takes His servants a long time to learn this lesson.

23

Divine Disclosure Answers

Whether or Not Our Request Is Valid, or Whether God Is Going to Answer Us, God Shows Himself to the One Praying

WHETHER OR NOT OUR DIVINE request is valid or not, sometimes God answers by showing us Himself in a greater way than we have seen Him before. Sometimes God doesn't answer our request; but rather, He shows us Himself. Sometimes He both answers and shows us Himself. Sometimes God shows us something new about Himself that we had not previously seen.

Remember the woman from Samaria who came to the well to fill her jars with water? She met Jesus who offered her *living water: "Whoever drinks of the water that I shall give him will never thirst"* (John 4:14).

The woman misunderstood the offer; she thought it was some type of magical water that would take away her bitter necessity of coming to the well to draw water. She said, *"Sir, give me this water, that I may not thirst, nor come here to draw"* (John 4:15).

What was the woman searching for? She wanted satisfaction and relief from daily drudgery, and some peace of mind. But the woman didn't really know what she wanted when she met Jesus at the well.

The woman said, *"I know that Messiah is coming" (who is called Christ). "When He comes, He will tell us all things"* (John 4:25).

Jesus' final answer to her was a revelation of Himself as the Deliverer who should come into the world, *"I who speak to you am He"* (John 4:26).

Sometimes our prayers are inappropriate. We are looking for things, or for healing, or for money, or we're begging God for an answer, but He wants to show us Himself.

King Uzziah of Judah had strengthened the fortifications in all of the outlying forts, modernized his army, revitalized the food supply for the nation, and gave Israel a long era of peace. The prophet Isaiah must have had a sense of satisfaction serving in the court of such a successful king.

Then King Uzziah's success went to his head, and he sinned against God Almighty. He went into the Temple and stepped across God's boundary between the priesthood and the monarchy. Uzziah thought that he was above any human priest, so he took to himself, the role of priest, and burned incense to God on the altar. Immediately God struck him with leprosy and within a year, he was dead.

We don't know how Uzziah reacted when his dreams collapsed, along with his monarchy. But let's examine what happened to the prophet Isaiah. Did Isaiah's dreams collapse when his king was driven from office? Notice what happened to Isaiah, *"In the year that King Uzziah died, I saw the Lord sitting on a throne, high and lifted up, and the train of His robe filled the temple"* (Isa. 6:1).

For what did Isaiah pray when his leader got leprosy? Did he pray for healing? Did he pray about a successor? Was Isaiah worried that the kingdom might collapse with a transition to another king? We don't know what Isaiah prayed, but we know God revealed Himself to His faithful servant. Isaiah got a *divine disclosure answer.*

Isaiah saw the Lord—sitting on a throne—and his whole life and ministry was changed. Any prayers that hadn't been answered became trivial when he received an actual vision of God.

Jacob the deceiver met the angel of the Lord at the River Jabbok and wrestled all night with him. Jacob the hard-headed, self-driven egotist wouldn't let the angel of the Lord go, so God had to touch him in the thigh with such pain that Jacob let go. As a result, Jacob limped the rest of his life. What did he say of that experience? *"For I have seen God face to face, and my life is preserved"* (Gen. 32:30).

Moses, the arrogant son of Pharaoh who thought he could commit murder and get away with it, was exiled for 40 years onto the back side of the desert. When he met God at the burning bush, his life was transformed. Better than any answer to prayer, Moses experienced the presence of God; and in the strength of that encounter he served God for another 40 years.

Sometimes you think you need physical healing in answer to prayer, so you continually pray, "God heal me..." or you pray, "Take away the pain..." and your main focus is the hurt that may be skin deep, or a hurt that goes to the center of your bones and the center of your intestines or a physical pain so intense your body pains your heart. When the only thing you want from God is relief from pain, for some, God doesn't answer that prayer. For some, He doesn't take away the pain, but He gives something better. He gives Himself, and when someone experiences the presence of Jesus in their life, pain goes away, and Jesus becomes everything.

LET'S PRAY NOW

Having God reveal Himself to you is better than any answer to any prayer you could seek. He is more valuable than any amount of money that you need. He is a better destination than any direction you seek. He is better health than any relief from pain that you crave. He is a better peace than any victory over any enemy. When you encounter the presence of God, your life will be transformed. What else matters?

24

Medical Answers

When God Heals by the Use of Means
(Medicine, Surgery, Therapy, etc.)

ON FRIDAY, OCTOBER 3, I finished shaving and used some Q-tips to clean the wax out of my ears. It's something I've done about once every other month for all of my life. But when I put the Q-tip in my right ear, suddenly I went deaf. I could barely discern talking, just noise; I could barely hear what people said to me. Something like this had never happened.

My first reaction was fear and terror; had I pushed the Q-tip in too far and punctured my ear drum? If I couldn't hear, could I preach plainly?

That morning I prayed three or four times for healing, and even when I did, God didn't seem to answer my prayer. "Lord, what are you trying to tell me?"

Nothing!

Then I decided to lay hands on myself. I had laid hands on others to pray for healing, so why not myself? I took both hands and covered my right ear, praying for God to heal my ear and restore my hearing. Nothing happened.

My wife went and purchased ear drops, and put them in my ear that night. I could feel curdling down in my ear, but I didn't know what was happening. Then I emptied the drops out of my ear and lost more of my hearing. It was like when swimming in the ocean and your ear plugs up with water. I heard talking like it was coming from another room. I panicked, and didn't use any more eardrops.

Monday was my usual time of fasting. I was praying for God to show Himself strong in the national election of November 4, 2008. I then added a request to my fasting petition: "God heal the hearing in my right ear."

As mentioned previously, when I fast I miss the evening meal, don't eat breakfast the following day, and don't eat lunch. I spend meal times praying for the petition that's upon my heart. Obviously, I was praying for the nation, but more sincerely for God to heal my ear and return my hearing.

On Tuesday, I made an appointment and visited an ear specialist, Dr. Hengerer at Virginia Baptist Hospital in Lynchburg, Virginia.

"Hmmm...," he said when he looked in my ear.

His "hmmm..." scared me; I didn't know what he meant. We went into the next room and with his instruments he began to clean out my right ear. Within two minutes, I could hear properly. All I had done with the Q-tip was to press the wax up into my ear canal which blocked my hearing. The warm ear drops apparently melted the ear wax and spread it around my ear like an even coat of paint covering my eardrum.

God answered my prayer for healing my right ear, not by a miracle or through supernatural intervention. He used a skilled doctor who patiently unpacked the wax out of my ear.

Sometimes God answers prayer through our frustration, through medical referral, and finally through circumstances. All of these factors were used by God for the healing of my wife, Ruth, during the summer of 2008.

In June as she was having dental work done, she developed a deep ache in the right side of her jaw. Ruth and the dentist were sure that a tooth was abscessed, or there was something else about the tooth that was causing the continual dull throbbing pain. So Ruth first had one tooth removed, then a second tooth, but the pain grew worse. It was no longer a dull throb, but became a sharp piercing pain that spread out like an electrical shock over her entire jaw. She described it like being burned, or stung by an insect, or stuck with a needle. She said that the pain was like touching the nerve of a tooth.

For the first time I saw my wife cry real tears, with pain. Friends told us about a young dental technocrat who was just out of dental school who understood the latest pathology. We switched dentists.

This young doctor sent her to a third dentist who prescribed pain medicine. It was an analgesic that was supposed to block the pain, but the medicine did no good. Ruth's pain began to spread.

We were prepared to go to an oral surgeon when both of us took off a week to travel to Davis College in Binghamton, New York, to speak at a pastors' conference. I would speak to the men; Ruth would speak to the pastors' wives. Then suddenly in the plan of God, the pain went away and Ruth felt she could travel with me to New York. She was able to speak five times in two days to the pastors' wives; we both believe God used her in a great way.

While there, Dan Rathmell, an executive assistant to the college president, took us out to eat, and when he heard of Ruth's condition he said,

"You have trigeminal neuralgia, or TMJ." Dan went on to describe how his mother had the same condition and suffered for almost three years before she went to the university hospital in Syracuse, New York, to see a specialist who used the gamma knife surgery to reduce pain.

We began immediately researching on the Internet through Google for trigeminal neuralgia, plus we sought more information about the gamma knife. It was there we discovered that the co-inventor of the gamma knife, Dr. Ladislau Steiner, MD, PhD, a professor of neurosurgery and radiology practicing at the University of Virginia in Charlottesville, was only 60 miles from our home.

When we called for an appointment with Dr. Steiner, we were informed that he would only see Ruth if she were referred to him by a physician. This involved a complete medical exam by her family doctor.

The pain was getting more intense all the time, and she was losing sleep and couldn't eat. Ruth was isolated at home and unable to attend church, school, or any other activities.

The day Dr. Steiner got medical information on Ruth, he personally phoned our home and talked with her at length on the telephone. "Can you come right now?" he asked.

We immediately got in the car and arrived there two hours later for a physical examination. Three days later she had her surgery; again, the hand of God was in the schedule, for if we were not able to go within three days, the wait could have been one or two months.

So what happened? First, out of frustration we left the first dentist and were finally rerouted to a third dentist, who referred us to an oral surgeon. We were praying, asking God for healing; but rather than getting better, her condition was getting worse.

Then God arranged circumstances to connect us with Dan Rathmell who told us of his mother's affliction with the same problem. In all of these situations, God did not miraculously intervene to take away pain, nor did God use the medicine originally prescribed to take away the pain. God used circumstances and referrals.

After six months, the pain was completely gone. I believe because so many people were praying that God heard the intensity of their intercession. And because there was a broad base of hundreds praying, Ruth was connected with perhaps the best neurological surgeon in the world to take care of her trigeminal neuralgia.

LET'S PRAY NOW

God answers prayers many ways. Sometimes He heals supernaturally; sometimes He heals through physical rest or exercise. Sometimes

He heals through medicine. Sometimes He heals through surgery. This time God used a combination of the above in response to intensive prayers.

What could we learn from these situations about prayer? That God sometimes answers with the use of medical technology or medicine; at other times with rest, or the opposite—exercise. On these occasions God didn't use supernatural deliverance, just trained specialists who knew what they were doing.

Next time you have a medical problem, you still should pray; but realize God may use one of several different ways to heal you.

25

Minutia Praying

I BELIEVE IN *MINUTIA PRAYING*—praying for little things. So as I go through life, I breathe a quick silent prayer for small things.

For big things, like $5 million, I fast for several days, agonize in prayer, and continually bang on the windows of Heaven to get the money, what I call a gargantuan goal. Not only that, I get as many people praying with me as possible.

But for little things I pray on the run, because I'm always in a hurry. When I drive anywhere, I always ask for God to provide me a parking space right up close to the door, and God usually does it. My wife knows that I pray for parking spaces, so each time we park up close to the door, she will say, "Elmer…God loves you!" She says that because God answers small prayers for me.

When I get up in the middle of the night and have to go to the bathroom, I always ask God to prevent me from stubbing my toe on a door or some piece of furniture. Sometimes I even remind God, "Lord…I don't need a broken toe; it will slow down my ministry." If you laugh at me, I hope you don't break a toe.

Sometimes I pray about such small things when I'm writing a book; I'll even ask what word I should write, "Lord…should I use 'awesome faith' or should I use 'extraordinary faith?'"

LET'S PRAY NOW

Too many people think that little things are unimportant, so they don't pray about them. But it's the little things of life that cause the most tension and anxiety in our lives. The old African expression proves true, "It's not the mountains that hold me back, it's the small pebbles in my sandal."

If we don't pray about "small things," pebbles will grow into mountains, and they will block our spiritual life and ministry for God.

So remember the world says, "The devil is in the details." But the Christian must remember that, "*God* is in the details."

When you ignore little things and don't pray about them, you begin to lose the reverence of life. Your life is made up of all things, both the big and the little. When you lose sight of God's working in little mundane things, it's difficult to see His working in the big things of your life. So whether you're stapling reports, waiting at a stoplight, or cleaning a kitchen counter, that's an opportunity to live that moment for the glory of God.

When I was a freshman at Columbia Bible College, I read about Brother Lawrence, a 17th century French monk who served at a mundane task in a monastery—he washed dishes. Yet even among the grease and dirty water, he learned to "practice the presence of God." I remember praying, "Lord, I want to be like that."

You can enter a sanctuary while driving on an expressway, or stuck in gridlock traffic, or sitting in a boring committee meeting. Isn't a sanctuary a place where God dwells...where we experience His presence? Each of us has a private sanctuary in our heart where we can retreat and practice the presence of Christ. We can meet God just as if we had slipped into a secluded sanctuary where God's presence is most evidently felt.

Once we make a decision to seek God's presence in everything in life—both big and little—we bring the experiences of spirituality to living.

Every little thing we do makes us what we are to become. Picture the little girl who hates to practice the piano. To her, piano practice is an interruption of playtime. But in her "little things" like practicing scales, this could likely lead to a mature pianist where her fingers dance over the keys. So, you can turn the mundane into a dance when you practice the little things that are important.

Therefore, pray for the little things—the minutia of life—because mundane *is* life and when mundane is elevated to the imperative, then life takes on divine perspective.

26

"No" Answers

When God Answers "No"

SOMETIMES YOU PRAY SINCERELY…you get many to pray with you…you even fast, but God sometimes answers, "No" because the request is contrary to His will. Didn't Elijah pray to die, but that was not the will of God? *"He [Elijah] prayed that he might die, and said, 'It is enough! Now, O Lord, take my life'"* (1 Kings 19:4). The same thing happened to Jonah; when he didn't get his way, he prayed to die. *"O Lord, please take my life from me"* (Jon. 4:3).

Israel sinned at Kadesh Barnea when ten spies brought back an evil report after surveying the Promised Land for 40 days. They said the cities' walls were as high as the sky, and that giants dwelt there, and that they would be destroyed if they went into the Promised Land. In contrast, Joshua and Caleb brought back a good report, saying that the land flowed with milk and honey, and that God would go with them to conquer the land.

In unbelief Israel rebelled against God. God told Moses, *"they certainly shall not see the land of which I swore to their fathers, nor shall any of those who rejected me see it"* (Num. 14:23). God promised they would wander in the wilderness for 40 years—one year for each day the spies were in the Promised Land—and that only the children who were 20 years old and under would go into the Promised Land.

When the people heard the condemnation of God, they changed their minds. The next morning they told God, *"Here we are and we will go up to the place which the Lord has promised, but we have sinned!"* (Num. 14:40). But sometimes just confessing your sins is not enough for God to change His mind.

Moses told the people, *"Do not go up, lest you be defeated by your enemies, for the Lord is not among you"* (Num. 14:42).

Has God ever told you "No" even after you repent of your sins, and even after you ask God to forgive you by the blood of Jesus Christ? Oh yes, God will forgive your sins, but He may not change the circumstances.

What happened to Israel? *"But they presumed to go up.... Then the Amalekites and the Canaanites who dwelt in that mountain came down and attacked them, and drove them back"* (Num. 14:44-45).

When I was fasting for 40 days during the winter of 1998, I had prayed for at least two requests during this 40-day fast. First, to know God intimately. The second, was for President Bill Clinton to be put out of office. I had no idea when I began praying, that the Monica Lewinsky scandal would come up, and that during my 40 days of fasting Congress would vote to impeach President Clinton. Instead of praying for Congress to be successful in impeaching Clinton, God spoke to me otherwise.

When I began praying on the first day, "Put Clinton out of office..." the Scripture came to my mind, *"Let every soul be subject to the governing authorities. For there is no authority except from God, and the authorities that exist are appointed by God"* (Rom. 13:1). But I felt that Clinton's moral life was reprehensible and that he should not be president. Then I read further, *"whosoever resists the authority, resists the ordnance of God, and those who resist will bring judgment on themselves"* (Rom. 13:2).

Then I was reminded of the Scripture to pray for those in authority over me, *"Therefore, I* [Paul] *exalt first of all that supplication, prayers, intercessions, and giving of thanks be made for all men, for kings* (Presidents) *and for all those in authority..."* (1 Tim. 2:1-2). God told me to pray for President Clinton to do a good job, not to pray for him to be replaced.

But I didn't pay attention to what the inner voice in my head was saying. I dismissed the inner voice because I didn't agree with it. So the next day as I began to pray against President Clinton, I again felt God speaking to me, "Didn't I tell you yesterday not to pray against President Clinton?"

I was sensitive enough to realize that it was God talking to me. So I asked God to forgive my impertinence and stubbornness.

On the third day I asked, "Lord, should I pray against President Clinton?" Again God told me almost sternly, "I have told you two days in a row not to pray against your president; why don't you obey Me?"

On the fourth day I was very tentatively coming into the presence of God. This time I asked, "God, are you really telling me not to pray against President Clinton?"

I received confirmation in my heart that I was not to pray against the president, nor was I to ask God to remove him from office. All this happened when Congress was going through a bitter debate over impeachment. While many of my conservative evangelical friends were supporting impeachment, I quietly submitted to God and prayed for God to use President Clinton to give peace and prosperity to the United States.

Think of all the evil rulers that God has used to accomplish His will. God used Nebuchadnezzar of Babylon (Iraq), Cyrus at Persia (Iran), Ben-Hadad of Syria, and other evil kings. Because God is more concerned about the holiness of His people, He will use an evil king or nation as an instrument to punish His people when they wallow in the sins of this world. Why? Because of the nature of God. He wants those closest to Him to be holy. Whereas an evil nation may be guilty of idolatry, fornication, murder, and all types of lawlessness, God expects better actions from His people. What sin is worse? The evil sins of an evil people or the evil sins of God's people?

When a believer should be worshiping God in his heart, but commits the same sin as an unsaved person—adultery, lying, lawlessness, and even murder—the sin of a believer is more heinous to God because His children should know better. To sin in the light is much more terrible than to sin in darkness and blindness.

LET'S PRAY NOW

God has many reasons for saying "No." (See Section IV, The "No" Answers to Our Prayers, Chapters 36-48 for a suggested list of the reasons why God may say "No" to your request. And remember, you're not the first one He has turned down.)

Then look at the many ways the human heart deceives its owner. Sometimes when we think we're absolutely honest with ourselves, we end up deceiving ourselves. *"The heart is deceitful in all things and desperately wicked, you can't even know your own heart"* (Jer. 17:9 ELT).

So when God says "No," accept His perfect plan for your life. God knows better than you, and God has a better plan for your life. *"For I know the thoughts that I think toward you, says the Lord, thoughts of peace and not of evil, to give you a future and a hope"* (Jer. 29:11).

27

Non Answers

When God Doesn't Respond to Our Prayers in Any Way

DAVID WAS CHASED BY SAUL for 13 years in the wilderness of Judaea. Repeatedly, Saul tried to kill David. The problem: David was anointed by God to be king, yet Saul—David's enemy— was the king. David was cut off from family, home, friends, and the house of God where God's presence dwelt. David continually prayed, but it seemed God didn't hear or didn't answer.

David the Psalmist prayed, *"Lord, ... Why do You hide Your face from me?"* (Ps. 88:14). Do you ever feel like God is not there, or God has not heard your request, or He's not going to do anything about it? Isn't that why David prayed? *"Why have You forgotten me?"* (Ps. 42:9).

When God doesn't answer, be careful of blaming God. That is what the psalmist did, *"But to You I have cried out, O Lord, and in the morning my prayer comes before You. Lord, why do You cast off my soul? Why do You hide Your face from me?"* (Ps. 88:13-14).

When you get a *non answer*, you feel as if you are in the bottom of a deep dark pit and you don't have any way to get out. You cry for deliverance, but God hasn't come. Then you ask for a shovel, but you don't even get the shovel. So you pray for God to say anything, *"Do not keep silent, O God of my praise!"* (Ps. 109:1).

Have you lost the music of your soul? Job cried out, *"Where is God my Maker, Who gives songs in the night"* (Job 35:10)? When a person has no song, this is a person who's lost his way, someone without purpose in life, or without friends—a person cut off from God.

If a young man is not sure about a young woman, he may pray, "Lord, I am going to call her on my cell phone. If she does not want to go with me, have her not answer because she sees my name on caller ID." But suppose the call gets dropped, or the call doesn't go through, or she's on another phone? The young man with a timid soul may lose his courage and never again ask the young woman for a date.

But suppose the young man has tremendous confidence. When he calls for a date the first time and can't get through, he calls again and again until he gets through. When the call is dropped, he tries again and again. Why? Because he is full of confidence and really wants the date with the young woman.

So when you get a *non answer*, and you're absolutely convinced that your prayer is within the will of God, then try again and again. Didn't Jesus say, *"Ask, and it will be given to you"* (Matt 7:7)? The original Greek says, "keep on asking." Why? Because Jesus promised, *"Everyone who asks* [keeps on asking] *receives"* (Matt. 7:8). So, your *non answer* from God is like a mirror that makes you look within your own soul. How valid was your prayer in the first place?

There is an illustration of *non answers* in Lewis' *The Chronicles of Narnia: The Lion, the Witch, and the Wardrobe.* "Digory's mother was dying and he prayed for healing. He had been desperately hoping the lion would say 'yes'; he was halfway afraid he might say 'no'! He was taken aback when it (the lion) did nothing." The answer? "The lion's face bent down near his own and a great shining tear shone in the lion's eye...he felt as if the lion must really felt more sorrow about his mother, than he himself."[1]

Is it possible that when we pray about something that hurts us, or frightens us, or is holding us back, that in essence God's *non answer* means He's not going to do anything about it? Rather than tell us "No," God just bends down to weep with those who weep. Then when we feel His sympathy, we can make it through any problem.

LET'S PRAY NOW

Sometimes it seems God is not telling us "No," but rather, God is ignoring us. Why does God give us the *non answer?* You would think that God would at least say something, that at least He would say "not now" or "later," but sometimes He just doesn't answer at all.

When you ask your spouse or children to do something for you and there is no answer, how do you feel? Sometimes you assume they didn't hear you, so you react negatively if you thought they were intentionally ignoring you.

We know that God always hears us, because God knows all things past, present, and future. He knows all things potentially and actually. We know that God understands our intentions when we ask. But would God intentionally ignore us?

If you send an e-mail to your boss asking for a raise, and you don't hear anything back, what would you think? You would think that he has rejected your request, or he is thinking about it, or something happened in the transmission—maybe he didn't get the e-mail. Usually, a *non answer* destroys our self-confidence.

Maybe your boss didn't answer your e-mail asking for a raise for a purpose you don't know. So God's *non answer* may have a purpose. For God doesn't do things haphazardly; God always has a purpose in dealing with us.

Perhaps a *non answer* is to get us to examine our heart more deeply. Maybe we don't see a sin that's there, but God knows all about it. Maybe God knows that sin will cause serious damage in the future. Maybe God's *non answer* will allow us to find that sin and do something about it.

Maybe a *non answer* is to get us to stop praying for something, because God knows He is not going to answer us.

Maybe God doesn't want to tell us "No" but He wants us to learn through self-examination that the prayer is inappropriate. We may need to learn that our prayer is contrary to the will of God, or we are asking God to break His laws, or it is the opposite thing that God has planned for us. Rather than telling us "No," a *non answer* motivates us to find out why God is not answering.

But there is a second side to a *non answer*. God wants our fellowship, and He may be waiting for us to seek Him with all our hearts. Perhaps our original prayer request was half-hearted, and God wants our whole heart.

Endnote

1. C.S. Lewis, *Chronicles of Narnia* (Boston: G.K. Hall Publishers, 1986), n.p.

28

Obstacle Course Answers

When God Gives Us Barriers or Difficulties
Before We Can Receive His Answer

FOR THE YOUNG MAN WHO says he wants to be a Marine, his sergeant makes him endure an obstacle course in basic training. For the young missionary who wants a college education, he must make it through Bible school, and then sometimes seminary.

An obstacle course has things to climb over, crawl under, go around, and walls to scale, water to swim, and ditches to jump, all planned to make the recruit strong and rugged.

Again, look at the young person who prays for an education to be a missionary. He must research, write term papers, cram for finals, pay for tuition; and many missionaries have had to wait tables, wash dishes, scrub toilets, and do a number of other menial tasks, just to get their prayers answered for a college education. In the same way, sometimes we ask God for answers to prayer and He gives us an obstacle course.

The young man who prays to be a football star has to go through the rigors, self-torture, and self-discipline of football camp. He must memorize the playbook and practice...practice...practice. The young woman who prays to win a beauty contest must practice diction, walking, dressing properly, and of course, she must work on the talent section of the pageant. She must do all this as she prays for God to make her a pageant beauty queen.

God did the same thing in the Bible. He promised to make Abraham a great nation and to give him the Promised Land of Cana. That sounded good enough. So Abraham obeyed God and left Ur of the Chaldees and when he got to the Promised Land, what did he find? The Canaanites were in the land (see Gen. 12:5-6). The land Abraham was going to possess was already possessed by someone else. God gave the land to Abraham, but Abraham had to use every talent he had, including working, fighting, praying, and even exercising faith before he could possess the Promised Land. And in his lifetime, he never possessed the Promised Land.

Maybe you won't receive the thing for which you are praying in your lifetime. Maybe all you'll do is begin the obstacle course to win the goal.

But when Abraham got to the Promised Land, it was not just occupied by the Canaanites, there was a famine in the land (see Gen. 12:10). None of us in the United States know what a famine is like. There is no rain, the streams dry up, vegetation turns brown, everything living begins to die; first the livestock, and then the wildlife, and finally the birds of the air. And you can't live on fish because there is no water in the streams. God promised Abraham the land, but he had to endure the Philistines and a famine; so what did Abraham do? He ran from the challenge of God, and *"He went down to Egypt"* (Gen. 12:10). Have you ever noticed that Egypt in the Bible is a sign of going into the world and that the way to Egypt is always down?

When you pray for something bigger than life, God may give you an obstacle course. Then it's too late to run away. Have you become like Abraham who runs away to Egypt?

If the Marine recruit stands up in the middle of the obstacle course and quits, he never wins. The same with the young woman in the middle of her college education; she never goes to the mission field. And how about the beauty queen? If she doesn't do all that is required, she loses.

Obstacle courses are created to bring out the best in us, but sometimes people fail. And how about the boxer? If he doesn't train properly, he loses.

But God is not a mean Army sergeant who wants to flunk you. No, He gives you an obstacle course to make you stronger, and He gives you the challenge of earning a college education to make you wiser, and He gives a young woman the challenge of the beauty pageant to make her develop her personality.

So when God doesn't answer your prayer but gives you the challenge of an obstacle course, is that your answer? Have you ever prayed for a summer vacation but ended up working on a farm? Is that an answer to your prayer? If a young man prays to become a pastor of a great church, he may end up in the obstacle course of a problem-filled first church. If he won't let God prepare him in a little church, he will never pastor the church of his dreams.

When God called Moses to deliver His people Israel from Egypt, do you think the son of Pharaoh imagined that he would end up in the backside of the desert tending sheep? What a humiliating obstacle course—taking care of dirty, smelly, disobedient sheep. But the lessons Moses learned in the desert leading sheep prepared him to lead over a million disobedient Israelites through that same desert.

Be careful! The bigger your dreams and prayers, the bigger the obstacle course you may face. A young man doesn't put aside his college cap and gown to step into one of the largest pastorates in America. No, God doesn't do it that way. The obstacle course includes learning to preach, learning to evangelize, learning to weep at funerals, and rejoice at weddings. The obstacle course to the ministry involves all-night prayer and fasting, plus the agony of betrayal, and as Paul said, *"besides the other things, what comes upon me daily: my deep concern for all the churches"* (2 Cor. 11:28).

If you know that you're doing things on a small basis, yet you pray for something huge—much bigger than yourself—then be prepared to run an obstacle course the size of your dreams.

Take a minute to think about obstacle courses. They're like mountains. You get to the top by taking one step at a time; you never jump hundreds or thousands of feet in a single bound. Climbing a mountain is tedious, so is running an obstacle course. So when you pray for something big, remember your prayer is only a beginning, but do more than begin. Determine that you will go all the way.

Have you ever seen the news reel where the Army recruit has to crawl through the mud on his stomach, then swing over a creek on a rope, then climb a wall that is straight up in the air? Think about those who design an obstacle course. Why do they add all the obstacles? Obviously, they want to test every part of the soldier's preparation so he can become a fit fighting machine for the United States.

Have you ever thought that God designs obstacle courses differently for different people? Your obstacle course will be different from mine, and my pastor's obstacle course will be different from your pastor's. God knows what they need, and He designs accordingly.

When you have a unique obstacle, learn the lesson that the Obstacle Maker has for you to learn. You may be marching in a storm through a muddy creek while I'm climbing on my belly in the hot sand in the desert. Remember, the Obstacle Maker always looks beyond any barrier to the goal. And the goal is never just to finish the course, the goal is to become a victor over obstacles.

Anyone who has gone through the obstacle course and won has proven to himself that he's a survivor, but more than that—he's a winner. He has proven something to his sergeant, and he has proven something to the world. Next time you see a service member proudly bearing his or her uniform, know that that person has finished basic training and was victorious over the obstacle course.

Next time you're struggling against an obstacle, look beyond your mountain to God. He didn't design an obstacle course to break your spirituality, but to make you godlier. Remember, *"God is faithful, who will not allow you to be tempted beyond what you are able, but with the temptation will also make the way of escape…"* (1 Cor. 10:13). Don't miss the part about *God is faithful.* Your faithful heavenly Father knows all about you, so when He designs your obstacle course, He plans for you to succeed.

LET'S PRAY NOW

Next time you pray for a large, strong, healthy body, how does God answer? He says, "Exercise routine." God will not do a miracle to beef up your muscles like blowing up a balloon. No! God's answer to your prayer is an exercise routine. You've got to hit the treadmill, after that the barbells, then the rowing machine, and finally pushups. First ten pushups, then 25, then 50, and finally 150. You prayed for muscles, but God says pushups.

When you understand the purpose of obstacles, you'll understand what God is doing in your life.

29

Optional Answers

When We Pray for an Answer and God
Gives Us More Than One Choice

HAVE YOU EVER NOTICED THAT when you ask God to direct or lead you, many times He gives you more than one choice? He gives you options. The trouble is, sometimes the advantage of each option (more than two roads to travel) is so similar that you don't know what to choose. Because you don't know what the future holds, it's difficult to make a wise choice.

But you've prayed and asked God to lead you, so what is God doing? God may be testing your sincerity or faith, or God wants to see how completely surrendered you are to Him.

Think of Ruth, the woman from Moab. She married a Jewish young man, then her father-in-law died, and next her husband died. When her mother-in-law, Naomi, decided to return to Bethlehem to live with God's people, Ruth was faced with a choice—live with God's people or with her Gentile family.

Let's go back to the beginning of the story. Because there was a famine in the Holy Land, Elimelech and Naomi left Bethlehem and moved to the well-watered fields of Moab. Why did Elimelech make this decision? If you know your Bible geography, you can see across the Dead Sea into the fields of Moab from Bethlehem. It was a case of "the grass is greener on the other side of the fence." So Elimelech packed up his wife, Naomi, and his two sons (Mahlon and Chilion) and moved to Moab.

The family settled in for the long stay, because they liked the neighborhood, *"And they dwelt there about ten years"* (Ruth 1:4). First, Elimelech, Naomi's husband, died (Ruth 1:3), but it didn't stop there. Mahlon and Chilion also died (Ruth 1:5).

Finally, God made Naomi so uncomfortable that she wanted to return home to the Promised Land and Bethlehem. Naomi said to her two daughters-in-law, *"Go, return each to her mother's house"* (Ruth 1:8). Naomi was like most people who are backslidden from the Lord. They have little spiritual perception for people around them. Naomi didn't realize that her daughters-in-law had a better chance of believing in the Lord and walking with the Lord if they returned to the Promised Land. In her unbelief, Naomi was blinded to what God could do for her, or for her daughters-in-law. Naomi almost sent Ruth back to an idol-worshiping culture.

Thus, we come to the option facing Ruth. She had the option of staying with her people where she knew the culture, where she fit in, and perhaps she might meet a young Moabite man and remarry. But she also had the option of going to the Promised Land where she could follow Jehovah and worship Him, but there was no option for marriage.

Naomi even encouraged both daughters-in-law into a life of un-belief. And Naomi said to her two daughters-in-law, *"Go, return each to her mother's house"* (Ruth 1:8).

Then Naomi complained of God's judgment in her life, *"the hand of the Lord has gone out against me!"* (Ruth 1:13).

There was something in Ruth's heart that made her choose the presence of God and follow the leadership of God, *"Entreat me not to leave you, or to turn back from following after you...Your people shall be my people, and your God, my God...The Lord do so to me, and more also, if anything but death parts you and me"* (Ruth 1:16-17).

Ruth made the right decision because she chose by using her heart belief in Jehovah, rather than the culture of her people and background.

When Ruth arrived in Bethlehem, she was a widow in a foreign country. What was she going to do? Since the Israelites were commanded to look after widows, even the widows of slaves and foreigners, Ruth could have rested in her widowhood and eked out a meager living.

But Ruth chose the urgings of her heart. Apparently Ruth was productive and she liked to work, sadly a quality not found in many young people today. Ruth's first choice was not to remain home, but to go out where widows were gleaning in the fields. Second, she chose a field that just happened to belong to Boaz. This is called the *circumstantial answer* (see Chapter 19) where God answered her prayer through circumstances and brought her to the field of Boaz.

"And as it happened, the field where she found herself belonged to Boaz, this relative of Naomi's husband" (Ruth 2:3 TLB). Then there was another choice. Ruth chose to work as hard, if not harder, than all the others around her. When Boaz asked who she was, the foreman said, *"She asked me this morning if she could pick up the grains dropped by the reapers, and she has been at it ever since"* (Ruth 2:7 TLB).

God led Ruth to make one wise choice after another and she ended up in the lineage of Messiah, and was the great grandmother of David, king of Israel.

LET'S PRAY NOW

There are many reasons why God gives us multiple options when we pray for guidance. If we were to pray for guidance, and God gave us a simple direct answer, our faith would not be challenged. If the choices were easy, we might even doubt His leading when things got rough, or the valleys became so deep we would think of quitting. But when we devote time to pray over several options, then focus our mind to make a choice based on multiple facts, our decision becomes more binding and we become more confident in God. You don't have the power to continue through obstacles if you have not made a determined choice to follow God before you first faced obstacles.

Another reason God gives us options is to test our resolve. We might be shallower in our dedication, and we might quit before we begin; so God strengthens our choice by giving us an opportunity to pray through our options.

Also, when facing choices we get other people to pray with us, or for us, in our choice. Didn't Jesus say, *"Again I say to you that if two of you agree on earth concerning anything that they ask, it will be done for them by My Father in heaven"* (Matt. 18:19). Options force us to take advantage of the power of prayer.

30

Partial Answers

When God Answers Only Partly and Does Not Give Us All the Things Requested

MOSES ASKED AN UNUSUAL PRAYER that God only partially answered, because the request was contrary to the nature of God. God has said, *"No man shall see Me* [God]*…and live"* (Exod. 33:20). But Moses asked, *"Please, show me Your glory"* (Exod. 33:18).

What did Moses mean when he said, *"Show me Your glory"?* Did Moses mean he wanted to see the glory of God at work again, just as God's glory was manifest when He destroyed the Egyptians in the Red Sea? Did Moses want to see the glory of God shining in the Tabernacle just as before (see Exod. 24:16)? Perhaps Moses really wanted to look into the very essence or nature of God Himself. Did Moses want to see the very face of God? That's the part of God you can't see.

The little boy asked his father, "Why can't I see God?" The father pondered the question for a minute and wisely answered, "Because He doesn't have anything to see." You see, God doesn't have a physical body like we do. God is not a man; He doesn't have a physical manifestation. The Bible says, *"God is Spirit"* (John 4:24).

But go back to that statement, *"No man shall see Me and live."* Would it kill us if we looked into God's glory? Perhaps God's glory is so bright that its blindness would penetrate us so we would die of pain. Perhaps if we looked into the very nature of God, His holiness would be so pure that our sinfulness would destroy us. Remember, He is infinite and we are finite. Therefore, for our protection we cannot see God. At times when God moved upon His people, He was like a burning fire and the people saw *smoke* (see Gen. 19:18).

So when Moses prayed, *"Show me Your glory,"* he was asking for something that was inappropriate and unavailable.

What did God say to Moses that constituted a "half answer"? God said, *"While My glory passes by…I will put you in the cleft of the rock, and will cover you with My hand while I pass by"* (Exod. 33:22). Then God told Moses, *"I will remove My hand and you shall see My back"* (Exod. 33:23). Notice, Moses was not able to look into the face of God. Maybe that's what God meant when He said, *"No man shall see Me and live"* (Exod. 33:20). God meant that no one shall see His face and live.

And isn't the backside of people the least attractive part of their bodies? The answer to that is probably "Yes." And isn't the backside of people the least discernible? We know people by their face, but very few people do we recognize when they are looking the other way.

God didn't show Moses His face, but He let him see enough of His glory that Moses' face shown for 40 days. Notice what he did, *"And whenever the children of Israel saw the face of Moses, that the skin of Moses' face shone, then Moses would put the veil on his face…"* (Exod. 34:35).

So what can we say about the prayer of Moses? God only answered half of his request. Moses saw God, but only His backside.

Let's Pray Now

Have you ever noticed that sometimes only half of your prayer is answered? You ask for God to get you to a destination—safely. And what happens? You have an accident or some other trouble on the way, but eventually you do get to your destination. So God answers only half of your request. You get to your destination, but not safely.

Every time I fly to a city to preach in a church, I ask God to get me there on time to preach. I get to my destination, but there are often delays, or cancelled flights, or a reworked schedule. God answers my prayer—I get to my destination—but not always the way I planned.

Why would God answer only half of our prayers? Sometimes part of our prayer is contrary to Scripture, while the other half of our prayer may be scriptural. Perhaps we have sin in our lives and God does not hear the part of the prayer that relates to sin. But the task we pray about is biblical, so God gets it done in another way, or by another person. Sometimes, half our prayer is contrary to the nature of God, but the other half glorifies God; so He answers only half of our request.

31

Pre-Answer Answers

When God Works Out Circumstances Before We Pray, So He Can Answer After We Pray

THERE IS A NATURAL PREMONITION between spouses who have lived together for a long time. A wife knows that her husband is going to ask for a certain shirt or a certain kind of breakfast even before he asks. The husband knows what the wife wants for Christmas before she tells him. This is natural premonition. But when God *pre-answers* our requests long before we ask, this is not human premonition, this is divine omniscience.

When God *pre-answers* our request, it's because He knows all things actual and possible; both now, in the past, and in the future. Therefore, because He is good, God begins to *pre-answer* before we ask, and because God is loving, He wants us to have those things for which we pray.

Eliezer, Abraham's servant, arrived in Mesopotamia to find a bride from the tribe of Abraham to be the wife of Isaac. Eliezer was looking for a "special" woman in Mesopotamia to marry Isaac. This is like searching for a needle in a haystack. Out of this large ethnic group of people, he was to find one woman suitable to marry Isaac. This was extremely important because she would be the recipient for the divine promise of Christ who would come through Abraham.

So Eliezer, not knowing how to go about it, prayed for God's guidance. He requested, *"Now let it be that the young woman to whom I say, 'Please let down your pitcher that I may drink,' and she says, 'Drink, and I will also give your camels a drink'—let her be the one..."* (Gen. 24:14).

Eliezer could have been confronted by a selfish woman, or a woman unfit to bear a son in the line of Messiah. But God in His providence had chosen Rebekah to visit the well at the time when Eliezer was praying—this is a *pre-answer* to prayer.

And don't forget the illustration of the donkey waiting for the disciples. Jesus approached Jerusalem on the first Palm Sunday. He needed a symbolic donkey on which to ride into the city of Jerusalem, a Near-Eastern symbol of peace. Jesus sent Peter and John to a nearby city and said,

> *"Go into the village opposite you, and immediately you will find a donkey tied, and a colt with her. Loose them and bring them to Me. And if anyone says anything to you, you shall say, 'The Lord has need of them"* (Matthew 21:2-3).

Again, because God is not tied to the cause and effect limitations of time, God provided a donkey which was there before Peter and John went into the city to get one. This is God's *pre-answer* before it was needed.

Think of all the things for which we pray that demands a *pre-answer*.

When we pray for a person to respond to a gospel invitation, think of the pre-conversion work of the Holy Spirit in the person's heart before he or she attended church. Think of God's work of conviction that motivates a person to get saved. Think of the circumstances that brought that person to the gospel service. God does all this to prepare a person for salvation.

When we pray for good weather for our event, or for God to hold back a storm, think of God working one or two days ahead of time to hold back or speed up a weather front that's rolling across the countryside. Before God answers, He begins His work of pre-arranging conditions that seem to the human eye a *pre-answer*.

Didn't God say, *"That before they call, I will answer"* (Isa. 65:24)?

LET'S PRAY NOW

When we ask God to do something for us, seldom do we think about what God would have to do to answer that prayer. We think like limited humans—we don't think like God—we just think of what we need, and we ask God to do it. Our prayer represents our human narrow thinking.

When a child asks a father for money, most children don't think of what the father did to get a job, or what work he did to earn the money. A child just wants money, so he asks for it.

But God is standing *now* at the place where every one of your prayers are answered. He's already there, because He is not limited by time; God is eternal. God also knows you will ask because He knows your need, *"your Father knows the things you have need of before you ask Him"* (Matt. 6:8).

So remember to be childlike when praying. Just ask your heavenly Father for what you need; He may already be preparing your answer.

32

Protective Answers

When God Answers by Putting a "Hedge" Around Us to Protect Us

SOMETIMES PEOPLE PRAY FOR THINGS that they think are good, but actually there is harm in the answers they seek. God does not answer their prayers because He wants to protect them. Perhaps some of the things for which we pray may actually be bad for us.

I planned to visit church member 94-year-old Katie Bowles who was in the hospital. That morning when I prayed I asked God to use me as an encouragement to her. She had been my faithful prayer partner for over 20 years.

"She left about an hour ago" the receptionist at the hospital desk told me when I arrived. I grouched a little bit—which is a sanctified word for complaining—I was grouchy because I had spent my time going across town to make a hospital visit, then found it was a waste of time because she was released. As I drove away from the hospital I was thinking of all of the other good ways I could have used my time in service to God. I even complained to God, "Lord, I don't like to waste time...."

The next Sunday in my early morning prayer meeting I learned of God's *protective answer* for my life. The lady had not been released to her home, but was rather sent to a neighboring town where they had isolation units in a nursing home. Come to find out, she had a very contagious infection. One of my prayer partners told me, "My daughter was the nurse taking care of Katie in the hospital. My daughter had developed a fever, vomiting, and severe shakes when she was exposed to Katie's infection."

Then, instead of complaining about wasting time, I praised God that I wasn't exposed to the virus. Not only did I rejoice that I remained healthy, but I rejoiced that I was told about the situation. Next time I will trust God more when He rearranges my schedule. After all, God knows best, and shouldn't we let God run our lives?

LET'S PRAY NOW

God's *protective answers* are found in the story of Job. Satan wanted to attack Job, but God had placed a "protective hedge" around Job's life. Satan couldn't harm him, so he complained to God, *"Have You not made a hedge around him?"* (Job 1:10).

Another indication of God's protective hedge is the guardian angels that Jesus mentions that were sent to protect children, *"Take heed that you do not despise one of these little ones, for I say to you that in heaven their angels always see the face of My Father who is in heaven"* (Matt. 18:10). Since God protects children—because of their innocence toward danger—can we expect God to send a guardian angel to protect we who are adults?

It seems Peter had a guardian angel. When He was put in prison with the threat of having his head cut off, just as Herod had done to James (see Acts 12:2), the Christians in Jerusalem were praying for Peter. *"So when he* [Herod] *had arrested him, he put him* [Peter] *in prison, and delivered him to four squads of soldiers to keep him..."* (Acts 12:4).

But an angel released Peter and told him, *"Arise quickly!" And his chains fell off his hands"* (Acts 12:7). When Peter got to the home where Christians were praying, he knocked on the gate. Rhoda, the gatekeeper, saw Peter but didn't open to him. She ran to tell the intercessors that Peter was at the gate. Because of their unbelief they said, *"It is his angel"* (Acts 12:15). They thought Peter was dead like James, and his angel had come to inform them he was dead.

God, who protects His own, knows when each of us will die. It has been said the man of God is invincible until God is finished with him.

So trust God; He will protect you until you die. Even then—when you walk through the valley of the shadow of death—you don't have to fear any evil, for Christ your Savior is with you.

33

Temporary Answers

When God Doesn't Permanently Answer Our Requests, but Sends a Short-Term Solution

SOMETIMES WE ASK GOD FOR AN answer to prayer, and He only gives a *temporary answer*. By that I mean, God answers our prayer, but it is not a permanent answer. In one sense every prayer has *temporary answers* until we die.

When we claim, *"The prayer of faith will save the sick"* (James 5:15), the answer is only temporary—that person eventually dies.

I was Sunday school editor for *Christian Life* magazine in the 1960s. I was not a Pentecostal but knew that the editor of the magazine, Robert Walker, had strong Charismatic leanings. Walker's secretary phoned to ask if I would come visit him in the hospital in Wheaton, Illinois, approximately 40 miles from Chicago.

My trip was a "journey of faith," because I knew when I got there Walker would ask me to pray for his healing.

As I entered the room, I surveyed everything and spied a small bottle of oil on a small table by his bed. I instinctively knew that he would ask me to anoint him; it's what Charismatics do. But I had been raised Presbyterian. Most of them didn't anoint with oil; and at the time I was a Baptist and most of them didn't do it either. (I later have anointed with oil.) I inwardly asked myself,

"What will I do if he asks me to anoint him with oil?"

I quickly thought through the Scriptures and couldn't come up with any reason why it was unbiblical. And sure enough, in our conversation, Walked asked, "Elmer, would you take that bottle of oil and anoint me, and pray over me for my healing?"

God answered that prayer and healed him, because as I am writing this 40 years later, Robert Walker is in his 90s and still very healthy.

A few weeks later in the office, he said to me, "I feel your prayers for my healing were more effective than any other." He went on to tell me, "Don't be uncomfortable with healing, this is what God does." He explained to me, "When you pray for the healing of others, God may do it; but don't lose your faith if later in life they get sick again, or even get sick again of the same disease." He went on to tell me that the body is susceptible to disease and sickness, and there may be a germ that brings the same illness again. He exhorted me to keep on praying for sick people, even when healing is temporary.

Paul got a *temporary answer* when he prayed for the church in Ephesus. He prayed that God *"would grant you* [the Ephesian church], *according to the riches of His glory, to be strengthened with might through His Spirit in the inner man…"* (Eph. 3:16). Obviously a man as close to God as Paul got his prayers answered. But approximately 40 years later when John wrote to the church at Ephesus, he chastised them because *"you have left your first love"* (Rev. 2:4). Paul's answer to his first prayer was only temporary, because years later the church was on the verge of backsliding. If Paul's prayers were not permanent, neither will be yours.

Every time a group intercedes for revival and God pours our His Spirit on a church or a country, remember, eventually every revival cools off. The great revival that Phillip brought to Samaria is not there today (see Acts 8:4), and the miraculous Christianization of Ireland by Patrick is no longer evident.

Look how many times in the Old Testament God's man prayed for victory over the Philistines, and God answered with a victorious battle. But the Philistines came back at a different time, in a different way, to attack Israel again.

The alcoholic struggling with drink prays for victory, and God delivers him in the winter of his soul. But sometimes that answer to prayer is temporary because in the heat of summer's dryness, he gives in to the temptation of the bottle.

LET'S PRAY NOW

What do *temporary answers* mean? They mean that because we are human, nothing in this life is permanent. We all get old and we must die, even though God answers with healing when we get sick. We all get hungry and must eat, even though God answered last week and gave us "daily bread." We all get tired at the end of the day and need more rest, even though God answered and gave us sleep the night before. Remember the promise, *"As your days, so shall your strength be"* (Deut. 33:25). God only promises us strength for one day, just as He answers our prayer to send us "daily bread." It only lasts for one day; therefore, we ask, *"Give us this day our daily bread"* (Matt. 6:11). And we ask, "Give us strength as our day demands."

34

Unknown Answers

When We Don't Know the Time or Extent of God's Answers

MANY TIMES WE PRAY AND never know if God answered the request that we seek. We don't know when God answers, how great was God's answer, or how broadly the influence for which we've asked.

Notice that we are told to pray for *"kings and all who are in authority, that we may lead a quiet and peaceable life in all godliness and reverence"* (1 Tim. 2:2).

We obediently pray for them, and we don't know how God answers our prayer, or if our president even allows God to answer our prayers through him. Not only do we pray for our country's president, we pray for our military servicemen and women of war, teachers, missionaries, and relatives that we don't see on a day-to-day basis.

I pray the Lord's Prayer every day after I wake up, before I get out of bed. Then I pray it again when I come to my quiet time. Sometimes I get stuck on the first petition, "Hallowed be Your name," which is worship of God. Sometimes I don't get to pray all the petitions of the Lord's Prayer, but I never forget the last petition, "Deliver us from the evil one." I know I have an enemy—satan—who would love to destroy my life. So each day I pray, "Lord, keep me from satan's attacks and from anything that satan would use to destroy my life and testimony." Then I pray for a "hedge" to protect me from the evil one (see Job 1:10). (See Chapter 32, Protective Answers.)

When I was a young student at Columbia Bible College, a missionary told the story of how God protected him. He lived among the natives in a crude wooden house without indoor plumbing or running water. Late one afternoon, he heard the war drums and knew that a nearby warring tribe was going to attack someone. He never thought it was him until suddenly he saw dozens of huge black bodies covered in war paint surrounding his house. Running from one window to another, he saw there was no escape. The missionary told his family, "If we die, let's meet the Lord in death just as we would be living when Jesus Christ comes." The missionary went on to tell his family that they should continue doing their daily jobs, right up until the end. "We will not cower in fear or scream for help."

The wife prepared the evening meal, and the children studied their books. Their father spent time on his knees praying for deliverance.

Nothing happened; the natives continued to stand in solitary command surrounded the house.

The family thanked God for the meal, ate their dinner, and when darkness came, they prayed and went to bed. Each of them expected to be murdered in their sleep that night, but they woke up the next morning to a bright sun and a beautiful day. The warriors were gone.

Obviously, God answered, but they didn't know how. Several years later the missionary preached in the village of the men who threatened his life. After several of the men were converted, they told of strong white soldiers with huge spears that came and surrounded his house that afternoon. The natives told of their fear of attacking, so they finally left. Then the missionary realized God had sent His angels to protect him, just as He promised. *For He shall give His angels charge over you, to keep you in all your ways* (Ps. 91:11). The missionaries didn't know how God had answered for many years, and the same thing will happen to us. By faith, we must accept God's answers, even when we don't know what He has done.

There's a story in the Old Testament of the people of God praying for protection from the Syrians who had surrounded a town. King Ben-hadad of Syria attacked the northern kingdom of Israel and surrounded their capital city for several months. Things were so bad that one woman had bargained away the life of her child saying, *"we will eat my son tomorrow"* (2 Kings 6:28).

Had the people prayed for deliverance? Yes. When the king heard of women eating their children, he put *"sackcloth on his body." Then he said, "God do so to me and more also..."* (2 Kings 6:30-31).

God answered when the army that was surrounding Samaria heard *"the clatter of speeding chariots and the galloping of horses and the sounds of a great army approaching. 'The king of Israel has hired the Hittites and Egyptians to attack us!' they cried to one another"* (2 Kings 7:6 NLT). So the Syrians ran away, an answer to the people's prayer.

But the city was barricaded and didn't know that God had answered their prayer. They didn't know their enemy was gone.

When food became so dire, four lepers left the city and went out to beg food from the Syrian army, thinking, "What's worse? To die of leprosy, or to die of starvation, or to be killed by the Assyrians?"

They discovered an army camp full of food, raiment, money, and livestock. The city was unaware that God had answered their prayer. When the lepers ran back to tell the city that their enemy was gone, their unbelief caused them to rationalize, *"Let me now tell you what the Syrians have done to us. They* [the Assyrians] *know that we are hungry; therefore they have gone out of the camp to hide themselves in the field, saying, 'When they* [Israel] *come out of the city, we shall catch them alive, and get into the city'"* (2 Kings 7:12).

So, unbelief may be behind our reaction to unknown prayers because we tend to believe only what we see. If we pray for our president and don't see an answer, we think God hasn't answered. If we pray for protection from illness or accidents, and we don't see visually the threat, we think probably God didn't answer our prayer. Our unbelief keeps us from rejoicing in God's deliverance, and it keeps us from giving thanks to God.

Let's Pray Now

I know there is a hedge about God's people, so I pray for a hedge for me and my loved ones. I believe God protects His people with an unseen hedge. I don't know how many times a drunk driving an automobile almost crashed into me, but God prevented it. I don't know how many times I ate something that could have produced an infection or severe illness, but the bacteria or disease passed through my system and I was protected by God. Did I walk through some bushes where I almost stepped on a rattlesnake? Was my hand near a black widow spider when I was cleaning out the attic? Or what about a deer tick that incapacitates one and leaves him listless for a year? Did God protect me when I didn't know it?

There are many *unknown answers* that we never know about. By faith, let's praise God for them now because we surely will praise God for them in Heaven. When we get to Heaven we will look back and see in many ways how God has protected us, and we will thank God then. Why not praise Him now by faith?

Remember, gratitude is the least remembered of all virtues, and is the acid test of our character. If we can't thank God for *unknown answers*, then isn't that saying something about our lack of belief in God and His ability to answer our prayers, even when we don't realize them?

35

Visionary Answers

When God Only Allows You to See What the Answer
Will Be Like, But You Can't Participate in the Answer

WHEN ISRAEL CAME OUT OF Egypt, they ran out of water while traveling through the wilderness. Moses knew the Sinai Peninsula, and he knew that there was water at Massah. But there was no water when they reached Massah. *"The people thirsted for water, and the people complained against Moses, and said, 'Why is it that you have brought us up out of Egypt, to kill us and our children and our livestock with thirst?'"* (Exod. 17:3).

God told Moses to stand before the people and use his rod to strike the rock. When Moses obeyed, water came out and all the people drank (see Exod. 17:6).

Years later, the people were wandering aimlessly in the desert when they came to Meribah. The people again complained that Moses brought them into the wilderness to die. What did Moses do? *"So Moses and Aaron went from the presence of the assembly to the door of the Tabernacle of Meeting, and they fell on their faces. And the glory of the Lord appeared to them"* (Num. 20:6).

This time God's instruction to Moses was different. Moses was not to strike the rock, but God told him, *"Take the rod; you and your brother Aaron, gather the people together. Speak to the rock before their eyes, and it will yield its water. Thus you shall bring water for them out of the rock…"* (Num. 20:8).

The Lord's command to Moses was very simple. He was to speak to the rock and water would pour out. But Moses was angry, or Moses was defiant, or Moses was proud; for he said before the people, *"Must we bring water for you out of this rock?"* (Num. 20:10).

On the previous occasion, Moses had struck the rock once; perhaps his memory overshadowed his obedience. This time, *"Moses lifted his hand and struck the rock twice with his rod; and water came out abundantly"* (Num. 20:11). Because God was merciful to His people, He supplied the water that they needed to keep them from dying, even when Moses disobeyed God in front of the people. Sometimes God blesses others through our prayers, even though we sin.

In the past, Moses had honored the Lord before the people. The Bible called him the meekest man on the face of the earth (see Num. 12:3). But now in arrogant pride, this time Moses disobeyed the Lord and struck the rock. The Lord said to him, *"Because you did not believe Me, to hallow Me in the eyes of the children of the Israel, therefore you shall not bring this assembly into the land which I have given them"* (Num. 20:12).

God forgave Moses, but Moses had to live with the consequences of his actions. Because God had spoken audibly, and everyone knew what God had said, Moses was not allowed to enter the Promised Land.

Then, years later, Moses tried to change God's mind, *"I pray, let me cross over and see the good land beyond the Jordan, those pleasant mountains, and Lebanon"* (Deut. 3:25). Maybe Moses thought God had forgotten His promise, or maybe Moses thought he had done enough to change God's mind, or maybe Moses thought "time heals all wounds."

Listen to God's anger when Moses prayed for God to change his mind, *"So the Lord said to me: Enough of that! Speak no more to me of this matter"* (Deut. 3:26).

We are sometimes like Moses. We forget our actions have consequences, and later we ask God to change His mind. We ask Him to remove the consequences of the things we did wrong.

I cannot tell you how many times I've been counseling with a young woman who has gotten pregnant out of wedlock. On many occasions, the lady has prayed for her pregnancy to go away. Whereas God may forgive her sin of adultery or fornication, God does not take away the consequences of her action.

There are others who prayed but God gave them a *visionary answer*. Daniel prayed for God to send Israel back to the Promised Land after 70 years of captivity. Daniel had read the prophecy of Jeremiah and understood that God's people Israel would be in captivity for 70 years (see Dan. 9:2; Jer. 25:11-12). So Daniel said, *"Then I set my face toward the Lord God to make request by prayer and supplications, with fasting, sackcloth, and ashes"* (Dan. 9:3).

Daniel even reminded the Lord that He had made a covenant that He would bring His people back into the land, *"And I prayed unto the Lord…and said, 'O Lord, great and awesome God, who keeps His covenant and mercy with those who love Him'"* (Dan. 9:4).

To make sure that sin did not keep Israel from the Promised Land, Daniel exercised *identification repentance*—he confessed the past sins of his fathers in previous generations that caused God to send Israel to Babylon. Daniel repented of his father's sins so those now living wouldn't continue to suffer their consequences, *"We have sinned and committed iniquity, we have done wickedly and rebelled"* (Dan. 9:5).

But God didn't answer Daniel's prayer to send Israel out of Babylon back to the Promised Land (although a few went back). God gave Daniel a *visionary answer* by showing David a vision of "seventy weeks" (Dan. 9:24). This was God's calendar predicting when Messiah would be born, and when all Israel would finally return to the Promised Land in the coming millennium.

Let's Pray Now

Whereas God didn't answer Moses' prayer to enter the Promised Land, God took him to the top of Mount Nebo and let him see the

Promised Land from a distance—a *visionary answer*. In the same way, God may not answer your prayer, but He may let you see the answer from a distance.

Many times men of God have prayed for a project and never seen it completed in their lifetime. But God gives them an inner vision—understanding—so they see in their heart the answer to their prayer, even when they don't participate in the answer.

Many prophets are called seers (see 1 Sam. 9:9), those who predict the work of God, because they saw what God would do before He began doing it. The seer sometimes saw the coming judgment of God, or they saw the coming millennial blessing, or they saw deliverance by God over an evil army. Many times the prophets saw in a vision what was coming but they never saw it in reality. Some received a *visionary answer*, where God gives us understanding or mental perception before a project is complete.

Sometimes you pray intently, but don't experience the answer that you seek. Perhaps God gives you the assurance in your heart that the answer will come. This may be an inner feeling, or one that you may see in your mind, which is called a *visionary answer*.

SECTION

THE "NO" ANSWERS TO
OUR PRAYERS

If you remember that prayer is relationship with God, then you understand why God says "No." It's because many of our "foolish" prayers break our relationship with Him.

Sometimes God says "No" because there is physical or spiritual danger, and some who are hurt turn away from God.

Sometimes God says "No" because we ask ridiculous things of Him. Doesn't a parent say "No" because of some of the foolish things a child requests?

And when you ask God to do something He can't do, or doesn't do, isn't that an audacious presumption upon your relationship with God? It's tantamount to a false relationship.

And every "No" produces limits in our lives, and there is no such thing as an infinite person who can seek limitless expectations from God.

36

"No, for Right Now"

SOMETIMES WHEN YOU PRAY GOD TELLS you "No." Yet in your heart you know the thing for which you have prayed is God's will. God has put a burden on your heart, and you want an answer to your prayer, but God says "No." What do you do? Give up? Turn to other activities? Pray on blindly and stubbornly?

Moses Turned God's "No" Into "Yes"

God had promised to Israel that He would give them the Promised Land (see Gen. 12:7). It seemed God's promise was finally falling into place because Moses led the children of Israel out of Egypt and to the Promised Land.

God would probably have never said "No" except that Israel sinned. What did the Israelites do that could turn God's "Go" into a "No"? While Moses was on Mount Sinai praying to receive the Ten Commandments, the people molded a bronze calf, made sacrifices to it, worshiped it, and danced naked in its presence.

What made Israel's idolatry so hideous? Three things: First, God said to Israel, *"You shall have no other gods before Me"* (Exod. 20:3). Second, *"You shall not make for yourself a carved image"* (Exod. 20:4). Third, Israel knew that God hated idols because of His ten plagues against Egypt's idol-gods. Israel should have learned a lesson not to play with idols.

But while God was speaking to Moses on top of Sinai, Israel was setting up a bronze calf and dancing naked before it in an act of worship. Because Israel repudiated God, He left them. *"I will not go up in your midst"* (Exod. 33:3). Then to make the issue even more convicting, God condescended, *"I will send My Angel before you"* (Exod. 33:2). Would you want an angel instead of God Himself to lead you?

Note that Moses didn't accept God's "No." Moses begged with all his heart for God to go with them. He determined to turn God's "No" into "Yes." Notice what it takes to change God's mind.

Moses didn't just ask God to do something, he committed his life, even his death, to pray as never before. Examine carefully what Moses prayed, *"Yet now, if You will forgive their sin—but if not, I pray, blot me out of Your book which You have written"* (Exod. 32:32).

Did you notice the dash in that verse? Nowhere else in the Hebrew text is there a dash—except here. English reading people know that a dash is a punctuation mark sometimes used to show an incomplete thought. Moses used the dash because no words came to his mind. He couldn't put his deep desire into words, so what came out? Just a dash. Have you ever prayed so hard and so deeply that you couldn't put your thoughts into words; you just didn't know what to say? The dash tells us Moses exhausted himself in intercession to God.

Moses did not just ask God to go with him. No, he begged God's forgiveness for the sin of Israel. Notice what he prayed, *"Yet now, if You will forgive their sin—but if not, I pray, blot me out of Your book"* (Exod. 32:32).

If God has told you "No," then maybe you've got sin in your life. How can God hear and answer your request when there's a barrier between you and Him? The sin of Israel made them unfit for God's presence, so He said, "I won't go with you."

LET'S PRAY NOW

So what must you do when you hear God's "No"? First, you must search for any hidden sin in your life, because sin not only *blinds you to its existence, it also binds you.* Sin *blinds* us to our broken fellowship with God, but it also *binds* us to our rebellion. What did Moses pray in repentance? *"You [we] have committed a great sin"* (Exod. 32:30).

When God tells you "No," maybe the problem is your ears; you haven't heard properly what God is saying to you. Or the problem could be your eyes; you haven't seen sin in your life. You need God to touch your ears and eyes. Maybe you need the eyes and ears of others to pray with you.

Moses got others to pray with him. Moses took his tent and pitched it outside the camp, far from the camp, and called it the tabernacle of meeting. *"...And it came to pass that everyone who sought the Lord went out to the tabernacle of meeting which was outside the camp. So it was, whenever Moses went out to the tabernacle, that all the people rose, and each man stood at his tent door and watched Moses until he had gone into the tabernacle"* (Exod. 33:7-8).

Never underestimate the power of corporate prayer. Didn't Jesus say, *"If two of you agree on earth concerning anything that they ask, it will be done for them by My Father in heaven"* (Matt. 18:19)? What would happen if all prayed?

Why would Jesus say that two prayer warriors are better than one? Because maybe Jesus understands the human limitations and frailty of the flesh better than we do. One person may misunderstand what God is saying, but probably not two people. One person can ask for the wrong thing, but probably not two. One person may ask in the wrong way, one person may ask too early or too late, one person may not have faith to move a mountain, but probably two will have it. Always remember, *there's value in the volume of prayer.* (See Chapter 8, Two-Pray Answers.)

Eventually, the Shekina lifted and God led His people from Sinai. God was again in the midst of His people. Moses had turned God's "No" into a "Yes." There will be times in your life when you need to keep praying when God says "No." It may be your sin that has shut up Heaven. One of the most noticeable answers to prayer is when we turn God's "No" into a "Yes."

37

"No, I Don't Undo History"

SOME PEOPLE WRONGLY SAY THAT since God can do everything, then prayer can do everything that God can do. But that first statement is not right; God *cannot* do everything. God cannot erase yesterday. God, who has invented time, cannot break the law of time, because He would be acting against the laws He made. And God cannot deny Himself.

There are other things God can't do. God cannot sin, God cannot tell a lie, and God can't save a person who refuses to believe in Christ. The correct statement: God can do everything within His nature that He wants to do.

Recently a friend was waiting for a big check in the mail. When she got the envelope she prayed, "Lord, make the check bigger than what they wrote." While this prayer seems to be trusting God for money, that's a silly prayer. She was asking God to do something He can't do. If she could have heard God's whisper, He would have said, "No, I don't undo history, the check is only as big as it was written."

God doesn't answer prayer that way, and God won't undo what's already done in history. (God can work circumstances today to counteract history, but God doesn't rewrite history.)

As the women approached the tomb on early Easter Sunday morning, they were bringing lotion and ointment to anoint the body of Jesus

Christ. However, their biggest concern was the huge stone that was rolled across the mouth of the tomb. The women kept saying,

"Who can roll away the stone?" I imagine they even prayed for someone to help them remove the stone. They didn't realize the stone was already rolled away.

The women were praying for something that had already happened. Why do many Christians wrongly pray for things God doesn't do? Isn't it because we mix up the things we want with the way God does things?

"I'm praying my baby will be a boy," a pregnant woman once told me. She wanted a boy in the worst way. I asked if she had prayed that way before she got pregnant. "No, I wasn't even thinking about getting pregnant."

It's too late to pray for the sex of a baby after conception takes place. Her prayers were wrongly based. If she had listened closely, she would have heard God saying, "I don't undo history!"

Some people equate great desire with great faith or great prayer. They want something so badly that they begin praying for what they want, not realizing they can't get it. It's as though God is standing in the wings to say, "No, I won't change things that have already been determined."

Sometimes we pray and God answers our prayer. But because there is a delay in the answer reaching us, we keep on praying. We keep praying for something that has already happened. Remember the imprisonment of Peter, *"But constant prayer was offered to God for him by the church"* (Acts 12:5). Note this prayer for Peter was probably made before he was released.

God answered their prayer in the middle of the night when an angel came to waken Peter. *"The chains fell off Peter and the angel told him to put on his coat, then the Iron Gate that led to the city…opened to them of its own accord"* (Acts 12:7-10). Once outside, Peter *"came to the house of Mary…where many were gathered together"* (Acts 12:12). When Peter knocked on the door, Rhoda who was the keeper of the door recognized him. She ran to tell the praying people that *"Peter stood before the gate"* (Acts 12:14). The prayer warriors wouldn't believe her and probably went back to praying. *"Now Peter continued knocking; and when they opened the door and saw him, they were astonished"* (Mark 12:16).

In the latter part of their prayer meeting, were they asking God to do something He had already done? Have you ever prayed that way?

Why do people pray for things that are already accomplished? Maybe it's because they don't know that God has already answered their prayer. When they hear that God has answered their prayer, they have such deep unbelief in their heart that they cannot accept God's answer. Isn't unbelief always the enemy of prayer?

I watch in amazement the show *Deal or No Deal* on television where people must choose a briefcase that contains an amount of money. Many people begin praying that the amount in the briefcase will be low, so they won't lose the game. Yet, how can God change what's already written on a piece of paper in a locked briefcase? If you've been in a situation and you've prayed like this, listen carefully and you will hear God say,

"I don't change words on a piece of paper that's already written."

Perhaps a man returning home prays, "Lord, let my wife be home when I get there." Either she's there, or she's not. God won't "zap" her from one spot to another just to answer a prayer.

The man returning home can say, "I hope she is there, or I wish she's there," because that's his heartfelt desire.

Hope doesn't make external things happen. Hope works in our hearts to give us confidence and relieves our fears. Hope is good when it helps us face events or a coming crisis. But hope is not the same as faith. Instead of praying for your wife to be home, you ought to ask for strength to meet the conditions of home, no matter what they are. That's a prayer God can answer.

When I was president of Winnipeg Bible College in Canada, we were a faith institution that depended on God touching the hearts of college supporters to send in money so we could pay our bills.

On several occasions I had to face my faculty and staff to say, "We don't have enough money today to pay everyone." Here's what we did. I asked everyone how much money they absolutely needed, and I added each amount up on a piece of paper, and allowed everyone to see the amount. When I had enough money to meet all the "absolute emergencies," I paid those bills. Then we divided the rest of the money equally among all faculty and staff.

On several occasions I prayed all night for God to send in money for the college. I remember praying as I went to the post office box, "Lord, help the money be there to pay salaries." Once I found only two or three envelopes with only a small amount of money. So I rationalized, "God, touched their hearts last night when I prayed, so it will take two or three days by mail for the money to arrive." (See Chapter 20, Delayed Answers.)

So the next two or three days I went looking for money, and on most occasions, it was not there. I died a million deaths each time my prayers were not answered.

Finally, one day I prayed, "Lord, we don't have money, what must I do to get money to pay our bills?" It's then that God gave me the inner assurance that I ought to be out raising funds among our clientele. But raising money was against school policy.

A hundred years ago, many Bible colleges and mission boards were called "faith institutions." They did not ask for or solicit money; they just prayed and trusted God to send money. The motto at Winnipeg Bible College was, "Full information without solicitation." We let people know how much money we needed for our bills, but we never asked for it.

God answered my prayer by *directional answers* (see Chapter 21). He showed me what to do; He didn't send in money miraculously. God led me to go solicit money.

At the next board meeting I didn't ask the board to vote on my idea to change the school's status. As a matter of fact, I just told them, "I am not going to allow you to vote on this issue, it will cause too much dissention and we'll end up getting mad with one another. Tomorrow I'm going to begin approaching people to ask for money."

I read to the board members from the autobiographical account of George Müeller, the man with the greatest faith since the apostle Paul. Many of the board members looked up to George Müeller and wanted to follow his example in operating Winnipeg Bible College. The problem: none of them, or me, had the faith of a George Müeller.

I read to them how George Müeller asked for money. He told people how much money he needed for a new dormitory, or a load of coal to heat the dormitories, or wagons full of vegetables for the orphanage, or how many head of cattle he needed for meat. Then George Müeller printed his needs in a booklet that included stories of one previous miraculous supply after another. To me, telling how God answered prayer in the past was a backhanded way of asking for future money. Müeller was just telling people about his financial need in a different way.

I explained to the board members that I was going to see a Mr. Gordon Smith, one of the largest brokers in grain futures in Western Canada. Two or three of the board members said, "You should have done that long ago."

I was prepared to take Mr. Smith out to lunch but instead he took me to his private club, and when I started to ask for support, he interrupted me to explain, "I only give $1,000 to every person from a Christian organization that I take to lunch." He had made a decision to give Winnipeg Bible College money when he accepted my invitation.

Our school salaries were so small that we could pay the entire week's wages for faculty and staff with $1,000. I immediately wrote checks to everyone for the past week, then said to myself, "Who can I take out to lunch tomorrow?" Then I began praying for God to use my luncheons for successful fund raising.

Winnipeg Bible College changed its name to Providence College and Theological Seminary, and is one of the largest and most influential evangelical colleges in Canada today. Why? Because a few weeks after Gordon Smith gave me $1,000, I organized an extensive fund-raising campaign where I assigned board members, faculty, and students the names and addresses of past donors on our mailing list (almost everyone lived within 500 miles). We challenged past donors to give to a capital campaign for buildings, equipment, and salaries for the *40th Anniversary Campaign*. At the bottom of the pledge card I added a little footnote, "Check here if we can count on this same gift next year." Almost everyone checked that box and God answered my prayer for money by providing enough funds to pay bills for two years.

LET'S PRAY NOW

Next time you ask God to do something, make sure you aren't asking God to break His laws (about time or space), or you're not asking God to go contrary to His will. Make sure the event hasn't already happened for which you are praying.

If you pray for God to send you money, make sure you give God enough time to touch a heart that will get that money to you. Don't ask God to fill an envelope with more money after the check has been written for a smaller amount and it's already in the mail. Otherwise, you may hear Him say, "No! I don't undo history."

38

"No, I Have a Better Plan for Your Life"

MANY TIMES WE ASK FOR something that is far inferior to what God wants to give us. Perhaps we ask for a morsel of bread when God wants to give us a hot roast beef sandwich. Or symbolically we ask for a drop of water to quench our thirst, when God wants to give us a big frosted glass of iced tea.

Elijah the bold prophet confronted Ahab and 450 prophets of Baal on the top of Mount Carmel. He believed in answers to prayer because he said, *"the God who answers by fire, He is God"* (1 Kings 18:24).

Elijah let the prophets of Baal try to first bring fire out of Heaven. They spent much of the day praying, dancing upon the altar, and cutting themselves to shed their blood to appease their god. But nothing happened. Then Elijah prayed, and God answered by bringing fire from Heaven to consume the sacrifice, wood, and even the water around the altar.

But Jezebel was not amused or intimated. She challenged Elijah, *"May the gods strike me and even kill me if by this time tomorrow I have not killed you just as you killed them"* (1 Kings 19:2 NLT).

Elijah ran away to save his life by hiding from Jezebel. He ran across the nation Israel, then he ran across the nation Judah, and finally he ran into the desert, ending up in the desert at the oasis Beersheba. Then he prayed the opposite of what he was trying to do—he was trying to save his life, but he prayed, *"Now, Lord, take my life"* (1 Kings 19:4). We assume this is a legitimate prayer; he was so discouraged, or scared, that he prayed to die.

It's easy to die when stranded in an oasis in the desert. Elijah could die of heat exhaustion; the temperature can be over 100 degrees. He could die of starvation; there is nothing to eat at an oasis. He could die of thirst in the desert. A clever band of Jezebel's cutthroats could have tracked Elijah down and murdered him. It would have been easy for God to answer that prayer.

God, who was listening in Heaven said, "No, I've got a better plan for you." And perhaps sometimes when you pray in frustration, God has a better plan for you.

God sent an angel to bake Elijah a cake, because he had a 40-day journey to Mount Sinai. It was on the top of Mount Sinai that Elijah would actually hear the voice of God. It was there the presence of God would pass in front of him. But that was not the better plan God had for Elijah.

When Elijah prayed, "Take away my life," God had an eternal plan for Elijah. Even though the old prophet would perform a few more miracles, and anoint Elisha to take his place, God had a much better plan. God planned to take Elijah to Heaven in a chariot and whirlwind, without dying.

Years later, *"Suddenly a chariot of fire appeared with horses of fire...and Elijah went up by a whirlwind into heaven"* (2 Kings 2:11). Elijah was going to Heaven without dying. Isn't that better than perishing in the wilderness?

LET'S PRAY NOW

If the rapture doesn't come, all of us will pass through the chilly waters of Jordan, which is called death. Some who read this book will die in agonizing pain, others will be killed as martyrs, some will die by accident or suffer excruciating pain, and some will die peacefully in their sleep. But we all must die (see Heb. 9:27).

But Elijah didn't die—neither did Enoch, who walked with God—these two people went to Heaven without dying. Isn't it good that God didn't answer Elijah's prayer to take his life? When Elijah was praying in the oasis at Beer-sheba, perhaps out in the darkness of the desert we could have heard the whispered voice of God say,

"I have a better plan for you."

39

"No, I've Got a Better Idea"

IT WAS A BEAUTIFUL, SUNNY fall day, yet a little cool. I was speeding down the highway for an appointment, not realizing I was at least 15 miles over the speed limit. Then I began tailgating a guy who was driving the speed limit—55 MPH. Since I was in a hurry I prayed, "God, make him move over." But God didn't answer my prayer.

Then I prayed for a break in the oncoming traffic so I could pass the slow poke.

I didn't get my opportunity to pass him. About five miles later, I prayed again, "Lord, I'm busy…move him over." Again, God didn't answer my prayer.

Then a state patrolman in front of the slow poke exited the highway. I hadn't seen the police car. Then I realized why God hadn't answered my prayer. If I had passed the slow poke, I'd have probably gotten a ticket. Perhaps God thought it was more important for me not to get a ticket than to get to my appointment on time. God didn't answer me because He had a better idea.

I was converted when I was 17 years of age, and in the church that night was a cute little black-haired young lady who was about two years younger than me. She was fun, caring, and full of life. I remember telling God, "She would make a great minister's wife," and we went out on one date. She gave me a portable radio that I took off to Bible college along with a color photograph of herself to put on my desk.

While in Bible college, she fell in love with a local boy and got married very quickly. She broke my heart and I blamed God, asking, "God, why did You let that happen?"

Years later, I saw her driving a rusty old, beat up Cadillac with her very plump arm hanging out the window holding a beer. Her petite figure had bloomed to over...I guess 200 pounds. I thanked God for not answering every prayer I made. Sometimes we ask God for our own selfish desires, and God says, "I've got a better idea."

My wife, Ruth, is absolutely the best minister's wife any servant of God could ever hope to have. She's a prayer warrior, encourager, filled with wisdom, and dedicated to doing the will of God. Ruth was God's better idea for me.

LET'S PRAY NOW

One of the greatest abilities in prayer is *trust*. We must pray with all our hearts, plus we must ask in faith and act according to the rules of the Kingdom. After we've done all we can to get our prayers answered, we must *trust* God to give us the answer that is His will for us. And what God has planned for us will be the best answer.

There is no secret formula to build trust, and there's no magical principle to learn to trust God. Trust is built on relationship. God wants a healthy relationship with you; He wants you to trust Him. The answer lies with you.

The more you learn about God from Scripture, the better you can trust Him. The better your prayer encounter with God in intercession, the more successfully you can trust Him; the deeper your relationship with God in intimate prayer, the stronger your trust in Him.

So, *"Trust in the Lord with all your heart, and lean not on your own understanding; in all your ways acknowledge Him, and He shall direct your paths"* (Prov. 3:5-6).

40

"No, That Would Hurt Others"

ONCE I WAS INVITED TO speak at a "peace" rally at a local church in South Georgia. Part of the congregation was "politicking" to get the pastor fired; the other part of the congregation said, "No...he's not done anything wrong."

The pastor had homosexual temptations or thoughts toward men. He recognized it was temptation from satan, but couldn't get it out of his head. He went to see a psychiatrist in another town a few hundred miles away, thinking no one would learn about it. The pastor didn't know whether it was satanic temptation, or whether it was a psychological neurosis.

But one lady in his church heard about it and before long, everyone in the church and the small community knew that he had gone to see a psychiatrist. Some wanted to fire him because he had homosexual thoughts because it was an abomination to them. Others wanted to fire him because he went to see a psychiatrist; they felt a Christian ought to seek answers from God, not a secular "shrink."

On the other side, many people thought, "He's not done anything wrong." And they even reasoned, "Our pastor is just like us, he's got temptations."

I thought I preached a great sermon that evening. I thought everyone was listening; at least they seemed to approve of the things I said. But as soon as the sermon was over, a business meeting was called and the fury of a storm broke upon that church. Some people were praying for the pastor to stay; others were praying for the pastor to get fired. No one prayed about the impending storm, or what it would do to the church, the community, or the pastor.

When people pray passionately against one another, what is God's attitude? Remember the Civil War between the states; the North and the South each prayed passionately to win; both sides thought they were right. What was God's attitude?

LET'S PRAY NOW

The next time you pray against someone, look at the situation from God's perspective. First, remember God loves everyone, and God has a wonderful plan for their lives. You may be praying against God's wonderful plan for a person's life.

Second, learn to turn your cheek when slapped physically or verbally. Jesus told us, *"whoever slaps you on your right cheek, turn the other to him also"* (Matt. 5:39). When you pray against another person, you are not expressing an attitude toward them that Jesus expects from us.

In the third place, try praying a blessing upon the person, rather than praying for God to harm them or for them to lose. Remember what the Bible promises when you do good to those who hate you, or you pray for them, *"in so doing you will heap coals of fire on his head"* (Rom. 12:20).

But there is a fourth thing: what does it do to your heart when you pray harm on another person? Can you step closer to God by stepping on someone else's head? Since God answers the prayers of those who are sincere, yielded, and humble, are you developing a Christian attitude as you pray for God to harm someone else?

Now let's return to that church where they wanted to fire the pastor. The pastor won the vote that night, but only by one vote. Because it was a divided congregation and there was hostility in the hearts of many, he finally had to resign the church and went into an interdenominational ministry in a nearby large community. God's blessing was apparently upon him because he built a city-wide interdenominational ministry that prospered.

41

"No, That's a Presumptuous Prayer"

When We Think We Can Get What We Want
From God Because of Our Strong Faith,
But the Thing We Seek Is Contrary to the Will of God

I TAUGHT A SUMMER SCHOOL CLASS at Baptist University of America in Atlanta, Georgia, in the mid '70s. As students are inclined to do, a young boy tried to flirt with a young woman sitting next to him. Over a period of two or three days, I noticed his pursuit of her affections became more intense. The more he talked with her, the more she obviously ignored him.

After class one day, the young woman told me she and her "real" boyfriend had recently sneaked off to Alabama and got married and they had not told anyone. Their parents didn't even know they had married.

When the young couple came to talk to me, I immediately told them, "You must tell your parents," and handed them the phone. They called her mother.

About an hour after the couple left, the young boy who flirted with the girl walked into my office with a bold statement of faith. He felt compelled to announce his intentions to someone, so he told me, "I am going to marry that girl, even though she doesn't like me now."

This presumptuous boy went on to describe how he could woo her to win her love. He had fantasized of her great spirituality that qualified her as an excellent pastor's wife—his wife.

I wanted to tell him how dumb he was. The word "stupid" crossed my mind. I wanted to tell him he was presumptuous about the will of God—that he was absolutely wrong. But I couldn't say anything because the young couple had not yet informed his parents.

Many people are presumptuous like that young boy—their confident feelings mess with their mind. They have *false faith*. They have convinced themselves that *what they want* is the will of God; therefore, by faith, they "say what they want," and think that sincerity will get it.

But what happens when they do not get the things for which they pray? They grow disillusioned. Perhaps they give up, blaming God, when it's their fault. *Mountain moving faith* is a biblical principle, but like all principles, it can be violated by human presumption.

LET'S PRAY NOW

There is a place for bold faith; we must be bold with our doubting heart and bold with satan's temptations. As a matter of fact, we must demonstrate boldness to many obstacles to prayer. Sometimes we even demonstrate boldness to God to show Him our allegiance to Him.

But we must always be careful that our boldness to God is not *presumptuous faith*. Note the meaning of the words. To *presume* is to suppose something to be true without proof, to take for granted. Sometimes we presume God will answer our prayers because we really want an answer. In this story, the college boy really liked the good-looking girl sitting next to him, so he mistook his desire for God's will.

However, there are times we presume God's will because what we want is based on the teaching of Scripture. We presume God will save a friend because the Bible teaches, *"God is not willing that any should perish"* (2 Peter 3:9). So we boldly pray and continually pray, or we almost have *audacious faith*.

Is it presumptuous to pray based on probability? Notice the rules for *presumptuous prayers*:

1. Always be cautious of your desires because of the influence of "the world, the flesh, and the devil" on the things you want.

2. Always yield your desires to God's principles found in Scripture.

3. Assume God is going to answer when your request corresponds to Scripture principles.

4. Pray boldly and with *audacious faith* when your requests are scripturally based.

42

"No, That's Not the Way I Do It"

THOMAS WAS NOT WITH THE other ten disciples who saw the Lord on Easter Sunday evening in the upper room. He had probably run away too far, and hidden too deeply. When Thomas finally came out from hiding, the ten disciples told Thomas they had seen the Lord. The doubting disciple said, *"Unless I shall see in his hands the print of the nails, and put my finger into the print of the nails, and put my hand into his side, I will not believe"* (John 20:25). It is a terrible thing to say, "I will not believe." But that is the danger of demanding a sign.

Many Christians have stumbled in their faith because they wanted God to do something special for them, something that is against the laws of nature. Some have asked God for special signs so their faith could grow.

Today people still want an experience or a sign. Dr. W.A. Criswell, pastor of First Baptist Church of Dallas, Texas, talked about hearing testimonies as a young lad in brush-arbor meetings. He heard a deacon say, "God sent a ball of fire out of Heaven that struck my soul." The man went on to claim, "I fell on my knees and cried out to God." The deacon concluded, "I prayed through until I got peace."

Young Criswell heard that testimony and tried to duplicate the experience, but the fireball "never came." Many people pray for a ball of fire, or they want to thrust their hands into Jesus' side, or some other emotional request. But God says, "No, I don't do it that way."

When the Lord appeared to His disciples eight days later, He singled out Thomas for an act of faith. He said, *"Reach your finger here, and look at My hands; and reach your hand here, and put it into My side. Do not be unbelieving, but believing* (John 20:27). But Thomas did not, as far as we can tell, actually put his hand into the side of the Lord, nor did he stick his finger into the wounds in the Lord's hands. He fell at Jesus' feet and cried out, *"My Lord and my God!"* (John 20:28).

Those who ask Jesus Christ for a sign don't usually get it. Those who ask for a ball of fire probably will never experience it. God wants people to base their faith on the Word of God. Jesus told Thomas, *"Because you have seen me, you have believed"* (John 20:29). But then Jesus commended others who believed without signs. *"Blessed are those who have not seen, and yet have believed"* (John 20:29).

Let's Pray Now

Some know the difficulty in their hearts of trusting God. They know they are sincere, but they also know there is unbelief in their hearts. What can they do?

Like Thomas, they can begin with sincerity. Since faith is coupled with sincerity, we must sincerely recognize any unbelief in our hearts before we can build sincere faith there. This is the same principle of the contractor digging away soft dirt so that he may pour the foundation upon solid rock.

When we look in our hearts and see unbelief, we should not despair, but we should be honest and confess our unbelief, *"Lord, I believe, help my unbelief"* (Mark 9:24).

Then we must go immediately to the Word of God (see Rom. 10:8,17). If we are honest to recognize our unbelief, and at the same time recognize our faith, we have a basis of overcoming the hypocrisy in our hearts. We are building our faith, because we've become sincere in our hearts.

After I graduated from high school, I spent eight years in college and seminary. During that time I took a lot of tests, and I'll have to admit, many times I prayed wrongly when I faced an examination. If I didn't study enough, or I was scared silly by the professor, I'd pray as I walked into the exam room,

"Oh God, help me get an A."

Most of the time God didn't answer that prayer. When I didn't study, I just sat in the room with a blank mind, looking at a blank piece of paper.

Once when I had not studied at all, I faced a 100 true and false answer quiz. I figured if I marked every one *true*, I'd make a 50. The questions covered a lot of "stuff" I never heard before. I prayed, "God, help me guess correctly so I can make an A." If I listened carefully I might have heard God say, "I don't do it that way."

Remember, don't pray against the law of learning. The time to pray for an "A" is when you are studying. Help God answer your prayer by opening your books. Then you can pray, "God, help me study the right thing, and God, help me remember the right things." Beyond praying to remember, you ought to pray, "God, give me insight so I can understand what these lessons mean." When you study and pray that way, you might hear God's whispered response, "That's the way I do things."

God runs His world by laws. God followed His laws of time, even in the six days of Creation. He created the world in six days, not in one second. Because God follows His law of time, you shouldn't ask God to go against His way of doing things. You can't plant a seed today and pray for fruit tomorrow. If you do, you might hear God say "Patience; I don't do it that way."

Sometimes we pray for people to get saved, but we don't plant the seeds of the Gospel in their hearts. Instead of praying, "Save Uncle Herman!" shouldn't we pray, "God, speak to Uncle Herman's heart when I share my testimony of salvation with him?"

And don't a lot of Christians expect God to do it all when they pray for someone's salvation? They don't make any evangelistic efforts to get a person saved, and they don't share anything biblical to get them saved. If they listen carefully when they pray for someone's salvation, they might hear God say, "I don't do it that way."

But still a lot of Christians don't understand the law of time. They pray for healing and expect it instantly. You pray for Uncle Gene to get healed, but he doesn't sit up immediately. He doesn't jump out of the bed and dance around the room like the healed cripple in Acts 3:1-11.

But wait, don't get discouraged because of the law of timing. Maybe God healed Uncle Herman immediately by eliminating cancer or breaking his fever, or removing a poisonous infection. But becoming healthy takes time. After a doctor cuts you open and removes a cancerous tumor, it takes time for the incision to heal and the flesh to grow back together. The cancer is gone, but it takes time to regain strength. God uses the time principle to heal the physical body. The next time you pray for a sick person to get well instantaneously, perhaps you'll hear God say, "That's not the way I work."

And what happens when you pray with wrong expectations? You lose faith because you think God hasn't heard and answered because He didn't heal immediately. God has heard and answered, but you can't see the results you seek. What happens? You get disillusioned and give up. Because you don't understand how God works, your faith in God dies a little, and your "hope" cools. Your wrong ideas about the law of timing have harmed your walk with Christ.

God does heal—none of us should be doubters—but God follows His laws to do things His way. God doesn't always do it the way we expect or ask. As a matter of fact, He's sitting in Heaven thinking, "I don't do it that way."

What should you do when God doesn't answer your prayers? You should say to God, "Help me learn Your ways, help me learn Your methods." Then you'll remember the Scriptures where He said, *"For My thoughts are not your thoughts, nor are your ways My ways"* (Isa. 55:8).

The next time your car is slipping down an icy hill toward a police car at the bottom of the hill, don't pray, "God, help me miss the police car." You might hear God say, "I don't do it that way." What you should pray is, "God, keep me safe in this accident, and please, I don't want a ticket." This happened to me in December 1954. God kept me and my family safe, but I got a ticket.

43

"No, You Are Basing Your Prayer on a Lie"

NO MATTER HOW HARD WE believe, we do not have New Testament faith if we base it on a lie. When Jacob was an old man, he was told by his ten sons that Joseph—the son to whom he had given the coat of many colors—had been killed by an animal. And the ten sons had the coat of many colors covered with blood to prove their point. The outward circumstances pointed to Joseph's death, and Jacob believed it. He mourned for 20 years, believing a lie. As a matter of fact, his mourning became despondency that influenced all he did.

After 20 years, the sons told Jacob that Joseph was alive. At first Jacob could not believe it. *"He did not believe them"* (Gen. 45:26). It is a terrible thing not to be able to believe what you are told. It is terrible to have a skeptical heart. Jacob still couldn't believe it when his sons *"told him all the words which Joseph had said to them"* (Gen. 45:27).

What does it take to turn a skeptic heart into a believing heart? When Jacob saw the wagons which Joseph had sent to carry him to Egypt, *"the spirit of Jacob their father revived"* (Gen. 45:27). Then Jacob believed when he saw proof in the wagons. Then Jacob said, *"It is enough; Joseph my son is still alive"* (Gen. 45:28).

Later, the entire nation of Israel was deceived by ten men—spies. Originally, twelve spies went into the Promised Land with a commission to bring back a report of what they saw. Their message became the basis on which the nation refused to enter the Promised Land. Ten spies said the Promised Land was flowing with milk and honey, but they also brought back a message of gloom and pessimism: the Promised Land had great walled cities. The spies described Israel as "grasshoppers," and the inhabitants of the land as "giants." The fear of the spies became the fear of Israel.

Israel could not believe God and refused to enter the Promised Land. They drew back in unbelief. As a result, every person over twenty years of age died in the wilderness. Why? Because they believed the unbelief of the spies. Their punishment was not just because of their lack of sincerity. Their punishment was because they wrongly placed their trust in a bad report. Sometimes a committee will say to the church, "We do not have enough money," and the church draws back in unbelief. On another occasion, the pastor has said, "No one is coming to soul-winning visitation, so let's cancel it." When the people believed the pastor, they did not aggressively go out to win souls and their spiritual life began to die.

LET'S PRAY NOW

When you base your prayers on a lie—something untrue—will God answer your prayers? Probably not, for God works in truth. When you pray for someone to be healed from cancer, but the doctor's report is wrong, God won't hear that prayer.

A lie doesn't have to be an intentional lie. It could just be an untruth. You pray for someone to be helped, but you misunderstand what you heard. You heard a family lost everything in a fire. But you should have heard there was a frost, so the family made a fire. You laugh, and maybe God laughs, but still, He didn't answer the prayer.

Sometimes your perception is wrong. You see a deacon from your church driving strangely, weaving back and forth in traffic. You pray for God's conviction because he is drunk, but maybe he's having the on-set of a heart attack or some other physical problem. Maybe God helped the deacon; not because of your prayers, but in spite of your prayers.

Between my freshman and sophomore year in Bible college, I worked as a carpenter's helper in a shipyard on a WWII aircraft carrier being refitted into a grain hauler. My boss sent me to the supply room to get an S-3 closet stretcher. When I asked for something that didn't exist, they had a big laugh at my expense. You can't get something that doesn't exist.

When you come to the Lord of the universe, make sure you are basing your request on truth—the truth of your heart, and the truth of circumstances. When you're not sure that your request is valid, ask God to "give you eyes to see" things as they really are. Ask God to lead you to ask the right questions to find the truth.

When it comes to basing your prayers on a promise from God in the Bible, ask God to remove spiritual blindness (see 2 Cor. 4:3-4) to understand properly His message in Scripture. Make sure to do the hard work of study, research, and memorization. Then when you know for sure what the Bible teaches, then you can properly claim the promises of Scripture.

44

"No, You Are Breaking the Rules"

IN THE WINTER OF 1960, Walter Splinter, the pastor of Grant Memorial Baptist Church in Winnipeg, Canada, was called to a meeting of the Home Missions Board for the Baptist General Conference of Canada.[1] Pastor Splinter was chairman of the board; he had to go to the meeting. This was an imperative meeting to determine the placement of new home missionaries.

Splinter had a small, single-engine plane he used for ministry, flying out to small towns in North Dakota, Manitoba, and Saskatchewan for revival meetings. God was using him greatly in these meeting, just as the Lord worked through him at Grant Memorial Baptist Church, the biggest church in the city.

Long before the Sunday school bus ministry was popular in the United States, Splinter sent out five buses to surrounding communities to bus children into his church. The ministry of Grant Memorial reached to metro Winnipeg plus the surrounding neighborhoods up to 50 miles away.

Splinter's plane did not have bad weather instruments or a radar navigation system to fly at night or through storms. The Canadian Aeronautical Aviation commission (the Canadian equivalent of the FAA in the United States) radioed to tell him not to fly because a storm front was moving in from the West.

Splinter phoned his wife to tell her he had to go to the meeting, and that God would take care of him. In the snowstorm he lost his direction and equilibrium. In a small farmhouse on the Canadian prairie, a couple heard the plane fly straight into the ground. Splinter was killed instantly.

"Why did God have to take him?" many asked.

But did anyone ask, "Why did he think he could break the rules of safe flying?" Just because we are doing God's will doesn't mean we can overlook common sense. And surely it means we cannot expect God to ignore the laws of nature when answering our prayers.

A small mission started in the slums of our city. The people met on Sunday morning and attempted to establish a testimony for God. The leaders were zealous, spiritual, and serious about reaching the neighborhood. However, they did nothing but pray. They felt that God would touch the hearts of the people to come in. But in essence, they yielded the progress of their Sunday school mission to circumstance. After six months the doors closed on the last service, and the building was put up for rent. Some Christians said it wasn't God's will to establish a testimony in their neighborhood. Was it because they broke the rule of advertising and outreach? Doesn't the Bible command believers to *go* to the lost and preach to them?

God has set His laws of communication. One person communicates to another through the five senses (sight, hearing, touch, taste, and smelling). These five senses are the windows of the soul, and communication does not go from one person to another except through these five senses. We cannot ignore this law and expect God to work.

Some Christians expect God to speak to others through a sixth sense. This sixth sense is something like women's intuition. They expect God to do this in response to prayer. However, God has set down laws of communication involved in speech, hearing, and sentence construction. He blesses His work through our efforts, not in spite of our efforts. The fullest blessing of God rests upon the fullest use of the natural laws of communication. The Sunday school mission failed because the people didn't communicate its existence to the neighborhood.

LET'S PRAY NOW

"Why did God have to take him?" the congregation asked about Pastor Splinter. The answer is simple. The pastor broke the laws of God. At this place, God could have performed one of two miracles. (A miracle is a supernatural transcending of God's laws.) One, God could have transcended the laws of the storm and caused the pilot to ride out the turbulent weather. Two, God could have raised the pastor from the dead. Either action of God would have been a miracle. God can do both, but few expect Him to raise the dead today. When we pray, let's pray in harmony with God's laws, rather than praying against them.

ENDNOTE

1. Story taken from *Christian Life* magazine, October 1965, 43-67 by Elmer Towns from original story, "Will God Pull the Rug from Under You?"

45

"No, You Can't Base Your Prayers on That Bible Promise"

WE CAN'T ACT ON A historical command given in the Bible to a specific person, at a specific place, for a specific purpose, and expect God to do the same thing for us today. When Peter asked Jesus if he could walk on the water, our Lord gave him a simple command, *"Come."* Does that historic command mean we can walk on water today? Obviously not!

Some people think they should be able to do everything that was done in the Bible because we have the same God who lives *"yesterday, today, and forever"* (Heb. 13:8). But not everything God said to a person in the Bible was meant for us today.

This chapter will keep you from praying wrongly because you misunderstand God's command or promise in the Bible. Actually, this chapter deals with correctly interpreting the Bible's promises connected to prayer.

We must be careful to understand the difference between a *descriptive command* and a *prescriptive command*. When the Bible tells all people of all time what to do, that's a *prescriptive command*. That applies to us today. When the Bible describes a local story in the Bible, where someone is told what to do, that is a *descriptive command*. The Bible is simply telling a story of what someone was told to do in the past. When they obeyed, God blessed them. When Jesus told Peter to come to Him walking on the water, that was a description of a miracle that God did on the lake surface. That is not a prescription that promises you can walk on water today (see Matt. 14:22-34). That is a *descriptive command.*

Jesus told the palsied man in the synagogue to *"step forward"* in front of the people (Mark 3:3). Then Jesus told him, *"Stretch out your hand"* (Mark 3:5). That was a *descriptive statement* of how Jesus would heal him. It is not a *prescriptive condition* telling us what to do for healing today. God does heal—see James 5:14-17 and we must follow that *prescriptive command.* (See also Chapters 24 or 42).

Every command in the Bible is written for your spiritual understanding of God, but not every *descriptive command* in the Bible is there for you to do today. You can't strike a rock like Moses and get water to gush out. You can't walk into a roaring river like Josiah and the priest walked into the Jordan River and have its waters roll back. Nor can you push back the Red Sea like Moses. We could also describe Samson with the jaw bone of an ox, Gideon with lamps and trumpets, or Paul picking up a poisonous snake.

God told Joshua to walk around the city of Jericho once every day for seven days, then on the seventh day to walk around it seven times to get victory. The walls fell down. The commands to Joshua are descriptive promises of how Israel could express their faith. We cannot walk around a wall seven times today and have it fall down.

But we can apply the principle to our barriers today. We can walk (actually or symbolically) around our barriers today and get victory.

While the physical command is not necessary applicable for today, our spiritual obedience is necessary. That means we must express faith completely in God to give us victory over our barriers and obstacles. We *may* express our faith by walking around an obstacle to overcome it, or we may walk around a piece of property to acquire it, but it's our *faith* that God honors.

When reading a prayer promise in the Bible, we must interpret every passage according to what God meant when He gave that promise. We must interpret the Bible with the question, "What does it mean?" Then we must ask the question, "How does it apply to me?"

There is a difference between interpretation and application. Bible interpretation is finding God's meaning. Application is finding how God applies the command to our hearts.

When I was a freshman at Columbia Bible College in 1950, I read the passage where old Eliezer prayed and asked for the Lord to lead him to the right girl that he would choose to be a wife for Isaac. He prayed that a girl would come to the well, offer him water to drink, and then offer to get water for all of the camels. When God answered his prayer, the Bible says, *"And the man bowed down his head, and worshiped the Lord"* (Gen. 24:26).

I felt as though the Lord was telling me that I should not be ashamed of Him and I should be willing to fall down on my face in front of people to worship God as did Eliezer. That evening about 50 students were milling around outside the school dining hall waiting for the evening meal. I asked myself the question, "Is this the time to fall on my face and in front of them?" Then I sensed the voice telling me, "Do it."

Then I heard another voice in me saying, "Everyone will think you are an idiot or some kind of religious fanatic." That voice said, "Don't do it."

The first voice said, "Do it, if you really love God. You shouldn't care what other people think."

I put myself through mental agony for almost two minutes, debating whether I should or should not fall on my face in front of my fellow students.

I'd like to tell you that I was a fanatic and I didn't care what people said. I'd like to tell you that I fell on my face and worshiped God. No, I didn't do it.

I'd like to tell you that I stood my ground based on firm interpretation of the Bible. But, like a wimp, I bargained with God and only went half way. I knelt down and tied both shoes while praying.

A good friend of mine was guilty of taking a verse out of context. Herb Dickinson, the best man in my wedding, was from New York. He read, the Scriptures, *"Go south"* and he went to Columbia Bible College in South Carolina. God blessed his life because he had a yielding spirit; however, one might question whether his faith was based on a correct interpretation of the command in Scripture.

LET'S PRAY NOW

We must be careful not to take the commands of Scripture out of context. When God told Moses to send the Ark of the Covenant into the swollen Jordan River, God also promised to roll back the flood waters. Can we expect to command flooding rivers to roll back, no matter how much faith we have?

The historical commands of Scripture are the *descriptive commands*. While we can't do what the original hearers did, we can apply spiritual principles today. We can go to the Bible to find the biblical principle of faith. Since biblical principles are eternal, they can be applied to the 20th century as well as to the 1st century. Therefore, our faith will grow when it is based on the principles of the Word of God. God does not expect us to walk on water today as Peter did in the past, but God does expect us to be obedient to the words of Christ as was Peter.

46

"No, Your Reasoning Is Wrong"

I BEGAN PASTORING WESTMINSTER PRESBYTERIAN Church in Savannah, Georgia, on the weekends while I was a student at Columbia Bible College in Columbia, South Carolina. Each weekend I went to the church, visited the homes on Saturday, and preached two sermons on Sunday.

The church was a large old Colonial church building with four columns on the front porch, a large steeple, and five stained-glass windows on each side of the auditorium. It was built before the days of automobiles and parking lots, so the church was built on such a small plot of ground that the water dripping off the eaves of the roof splashed on the neighbor's property.

Each time it would rain, I went to a certain window in the church to look out and pray that we could obtain the four city lots next door.

The more I prayed for the city lots, the stronger my anticipation became to get them. I just had to have those lots for the church, so I prayed more vehemently and more deeply.

I even had a vision of what I would do with those four lots. I planned to build an L-shaped building with the porch running the length of the building on the inside of the L.

One time I decided to walk the perimeter of the four lots and claim them by faith. After all, God had told Abraham to walk through the Promised Land and claim it: *"Arise, walk through the land in the length of it and in the breadth of it; for I will give it unto thee"* (Gen. 13:17).

The only problem was weeds growing on the end lot up against the fencing of chicken wire of a neighboring house. I was pushing the weeds aside trying to walk the property to pray when the neighbor came out and yelled, "Preacher, what are you doing walking through the weeds?" I was too embarrassed to tell him what I was doing.

"Come, walk through the yard," the neighbor said to me.

The church never got those lots, and my prayers were never answered. Years later I went back to visit the church and found four small homes built on those lots. I realized my prayers would never be answered.

Let's Pray Now

Perhaps God looked down from Heaven and knew I would only be in that church about a year, so He didn't answer because I would never build on those lots. Perhaps there were other considerations. Was God saying, "No, your reasoning is wrong"?

I found out that the lots only cost $100 each. Later, I became a college president and on several occasions bought property and sold it. I realized that $100 was almost nothing to purchase property. My reasoning was immature.

What would I do today? I'd get a realtor, write a contract on those lots, and go before the church to ask for individuals to give me $100 each to purchase a lot for church expansion. There are many different ways to raise money and pay for church expansion, but because of my immaturity and faulty reasoning, I didn't capitalize on any of them.

47

"No, You Are Not Mature Enough"

THE FIRST SERMON I EVER preached was a "bust." If you don't understand the word "bust," think of "flop," or "an embarrassment."

I was too young to be a great, strong preacher, and I was too immature to experience the power of God. But God took a "failed" sermon and brought a multitude to Jesus Christ.

When I first went to Columbia Bible College, I attended Saturday night street meetings in downtown Columbia, South Carolina. These meetings were mostly made up of soldiers from nearby Fort Jackson. On Saturday evenings, they walked the streets of Columbia with nothing to do. Usually, seven or eight of us from the Bible college would fan out and each try to "capture" a group of three or four soldiers and bring them back to the street meeting.

As a result, we usually had a street meeting of around 20 people, mostly young soldiers.

Seven or eight students took turns, each one preaching on a Saturday night. I worked diligently, thinking my time to preach would come, even though I would be the last in line. But they didn't give me an opportunity to preach after everyone preached because I was only a freshman. They started through the cycle again.

I faithfully worked every Saturday night that I was in town. It was my way of serving God.

In February 1951, it was finally my time to preach. I knew about a week in advance that I was assigned to preach. Gladdie Kreimann was chosen to lead singing. We decided to skip our lunch every day for a week and go to the prayer room at Legsters Hall on the men's campus to pray for one hour for the street meeting.

We met faithfully for one hour, Monday through Friday, asking God to pour out His power on the street meeting. We claimed God's promise, *"If two of you agree on earth concerning anything that they ask, it will be done for them by My Father in heaven"* (Matt. 18:19).

When it was my time to preach, it was a blustery, cold Saturday evening with a nip of moisture in the air. Only three students showed up; one boy to play the pump organ, Gladdie to lead singing, and me to preach. Immediately I knew the crowd would be small, but didn't know how small.

The organ player stayed with the organ, while Gladdie and I went to round up soldiers; but because it was bitter cold, only four or five soldiers came back to the street meeting. Usually, we sang three or four well-known hymns that most of the Army recruits would know from any casual contact they had with the church. But this evening, because it was cold, Gladdie led in only one song and almost no one sang. Then he led in prayer, and told me to preach.

I was caught by surprise, but that's not the reason the sermon flopped. I had prepared faithfully, but that's not the reason the sermon flopped. I just didn't have the maturity to handle the situation. My sermon was based on Matthew 7:13-14, *"Enter by the narrow gate; for wide is the gate and broad is the way that leads to destruction, and there are many who go in by it. Because narrow is the gate and difficult is the way which leads to life, and there are few who find it."*

I had preached the sermon three or four times in my dormitory room to a full-length mirror. I remember it took almost 15 minutes to preach the sermon, but that night I finished in less than three minutes. So I repeated the sermon a second time; and only five minutes were gone.

"What am I gonna do?" I panicked.

I gave an invitation to come forward to the four or five young recruits who were standing less than 5 feet from me. It was an embarrassing situation as we sang, "Just as I am." When nothing happened, I asked them to bow their heads and I began to pray the benediction. As I said, "Amen," I heard a loud bellow from the back.

"MAY I SAY A WORD...?"

And looking up I saw this huge American Indian dressed in buckskin who stood at least 6 feet 9 inches tall, like a menacing linebacker. He moved quickly to the front and center and bellowed again,

"MAY I SAY A WORD...?"

His request was a command, and we all stood at attention as he quoted an entire chapter out of Isaiah on the millennium, the thousand-year reign of Christ. His voice, his piercing eyes, and his huge gestures captivated the seven of us who stood, daring not to move.

I was intrigued; he stood on his tiptoes to preach. He would tiptoe toward the audience and then when he captivated us with his eyes, he moved back pulling the crowd with him. What I didn't realize was that he was pulling us away from the street corner so that he could gather more people.

Everyone who walked by stopped to listen. Drivers in cars passing through the intersection stopped on both sides of the street with rolled-down windows. Before I knew it, cars were double parked on both sides of the street, backed up three or four deep, listening to this powerful presentation of the gospel of Jesus Christ. I hung on every word, sensing the anointing of God on his words as they captured the hearts of the listening crowd. Now almost 40 or 50 people listened—captivated.

After a sermon that seemed more than 30 minutes long, his finger pointed almost to the dusty sidewalk as he yelled,

"KNEEL...KNEEL...KNEEL!"

Young men dropped to their knees, and just as quickly, I knelt by their side on my knees with an open Bible. I led one soldier to Christ, and without getting up I crawled on my knees over to the next, and led him to Christ. The two boys from Columbia Bible College were quickly leading soldiers to Christ, one at a time. When I had led the last soldier to Christ and there was no one else, I looked around and saw the evangelist was gone. The giant man with high cheek bones and black greasy hair combed straight back was gone. I looked in every direction to find him, but he was gone.

Let's Pray Now

What can I make of my first sermon? I think God looked down from Heaven and saw Elmer and Gladdie praying every day during lunch hour, begging for an anointing on their first street meeting. When God realized that both young boys were too immature, God had His servant—an Indian evangelist—ready and willing to preach the Gospel.

I learned a lesson of yieldedness from this experience. Even when you've prayed as deeply as you can—yielding everything to God—He may use someone else to answer your prayer. Why? Because they can do the job better than you.

I also learned the lesson of humility in this experience. Sometimes when I'm not mature enough for the power of God, I wait for God to use someone else to accomplish what I couldn't do. It's amazing what you can do for God if you don't care who gets the credit.

48

"No, You've Got to Be Kidding"

I 'VE HEARD PEOPLE PRAY WHAT I call "foolish prayers." When I was a freshman in Bible college, there was a fellow freshman who was absolutely convinced that he could fly if he had enough faith. We got into this argument because one of our teachers said, "Man can't fly, no matter how much faith he has." But my fellow freshman said,

"If I really have faith, and pray long enough, and have absolute trust in God, I could fly."

First, my classmates argued with him. After a while we laughed at him. Then one week he attempted to fly. He first prayed, "Lord, help Thou my unbelief." I was not there when it happened, but a bunch of guys were standing around in the lobby of the men's dorm—I think—teasing him about his claim.

The "air-walker" worked himself up to such a pitch that he finally said, "I'll do it now." He stood on a chair, prayed sincerely, then took his leap of faith into the air. His first step hit the floor.

If you had seen God watching, the Deity might have said, "He's got to be kidding."

What does God say when we pray for things that are contrary to His nature? *"God made birds to fly, and then He reproduced them after their kind"* (see Gen. 1:21). We're not birds, we're humans, made after our kind, and God placed the limitation of gravity upon us.

So the next time you hear a human say, "I can fly," listen carefully and you might hear God's reply, "You've got to be kidding."

Don't pray against God's law of growth. When a baby is one week old, would you expect the child to get up and run…? No! Suppose a proud father prayed for his newborn baby to run. We shouldn't laugh at his misplaced faith, even though it is foolish faith. Also, we shouldn't ask God to honor his prayers, even though the father has no grounds for the prayer he makes.

So the next time you hear a father praying for his newborn son to run, or when another father prays for his junior high school boy to win the NCAA track meet, listen carefully to the voice of God in Heaven, "You've got to be kidding."

Also, don't pray against the law of learning. There are many things we can't do until we learn. Suppose someone prayed for a newborn Christian to preach a powerful biblical sermon to an audience of 30,000.

Some may ask, "Wouldn't that please the Father?" Yes, but that's not the way God does it. We live with our limitation of ignorance, and God will help us overcome our ignorance if we read, memorize, listen to others, respond, and apply ourselves.

There's a problem with praying for a newborn Christian to preach a powerful sermon. The newborn Christian doesn't know much about the Bible, and he may not know much about human psychology or how to motivate people; he may not even know much about the power of God and spiritual anointing, or how to motivate a great audience to make spiritual decisions. Those are things that must be learned by a young pastor, and some of those things are acquired by many years of ministry.

So the next time you think about a brand-new Christian preaching a great biblical sermon to an audience, listen for the voice of God:

"You've got to be kidding."

And there is another thing. Don't pray against God's law of time. A lady in her late twenties came to see me because she was pregnant out of wedlock. She had been hiding it from her family and friends, but was beginning to show. She prayed seriously for God to take away her baby. As I questioned her thoroughly, I learned she never wanted an abortion, nor did she want the baby dead. She just wanted it to go away. Obviously, she was a naïve Christian. God doesn't undo history.

"But God can do anything," she told me through her sobs. "Why doesn't God answer this prayer?"

LET'S PRAY NOW

God won't erase yesterday and God won't go back to blot out the past. Now, God forgives the sins of the past, but He won't make a pregnant woman not pregnant.

We live today and we look forward to tomorrow. The only thing that the past has for us are lessons and the foundation for the future. We can learn from the past but we can't change it.

The next time you hear someone praying for God to change the actions of the past, listen for God, who says, "You've got to be kidding."

But let's not close on a negative note. Whereas God won't erase our mistakes, He will forgive our past sins and separate them as far as the East is from the West, and remember them no more.

EPILOGUE

Understanding Answers

Answer: \'an(t)-sər\ root: a prehistoric compound, first to join with the one asking, and second, to swear. Meaning, (1) reply to a question or request; (2) rejoinder to a charge, (3) respond to an act, (4) to conform to a request. Syn.— reply, retort, rejoinder, response, conform, reject, return.

This book is about answers—how God answers prayer. Whereas most books on prayer focus on the one praying, this book has analyzed how God answers. Now that you understand how God answers, you'll be better able to pray.

Have you ever noticed how you answer differently according to the person who calls you? You are surprised when someone calls your name in a crowd. You answer with irritation a telephone call from an unwanted solicitor. You answer impersonally to a business e-mail. You debate when the other is wrong. You defend when attacked. These are only a few ways you answer.

So don't be surprised when God answers differently to all the various ways that we pray to Him. This book explained 48 different ways God answers our prayers.

When you understand *How God Answers Prayer*, you will have more success in your intercession because you will know how to properly ask God for the things you want.

Most books look at prayer from the front end—before you pray. This book looked at final results—how God answers after you pray. Where does God answer? When does God answer? Or why don't we get what we request?

Did you know the word *answers* is not found very often in the Bible? It's not mentioned nearly as often as the word *pray*. While many have written books on prayer, not many people have written books on answers. Why is that? Maybe we're self-centered and think only of ourselves when we pray. But shouldn't prayer be focused on God, the One to whom we're speaking?

This book was written on the premise that God not only answers intercessory prayer, but He answers in many ways. One of the first occurrences of the word *answer* in Scripture is a reference to Jacob who built an altar unto God, saying, *"I will make an altar there to God, who answered me in the day of my distress and has been with me in the way which I have gone"* (Gen. 35:3). How did Jacob get an answer from God? He originally asked for God to *"be with me, and keep me in this way that I am going, and give me bread to eat and clothing to put on, so that I come back to my father's house in peace"* (Gen. 28:20-21). Because God answered Jacob's prayer, he built an altar and sacrificed to God.

On many occasions throughout the sufferings of Job, he asked God to explain why he was in pain or why so many bad things happened to him. Finally, *"the Lord answered Job out of the whirlwind"* (Job 38:1; 40:1). (See Chapter 20 on Delayed Answers.)

Moses, Aaron, Samuel, and the priest, *"called upon the Lord, and He answered them"* (Ps. 99:6). See also Chapter 1 (Asking Answers— Blind Bartimaeus Factor) where God hears those who ask for answers.

Then Elijah confronted the false priests of Balaam with the challenge, *"The God who answers by fire, He is God"* (1 Kings 18:24).

So God's people—like Elijah—expect answers to their intercessory prayers. That's why the Psalmist begged, *"You will answer us, O God"* (Ps. 65:5).

One of God's greatest invitations in the Bible is *"Call to Me, and I will answer you"* (Jer. 33:3). God in Heaven challenges us to "call on Him." He has promised, *"I will answer."*

We have the assurance that God knows our need before we ask (see Matt 6:8), and that He has put things in motion: *"Before they call, I will answer"* (Isa. 65:24).

ABOUT THE AUTHOR

Dr. Elmer Towns is an author of popular and scholarly works, a seminar lecturer, and a dedicated worker in Sunday school. He has written over 125 books, including several best sellers. He won the coveted Gold Medallion Book Award for *The Names of the Holy Spirit*.

Dr. Elmer Towns also cofounded Liberty University with Jerry Falwell in 1971 and now serves as Dean of the B.R. Lakin School of Religion and as professor of Theology and New Testament.

Liberty University was founded in 1971 and is the fastest growing Christian university in America. Located in Lynchburg, Virginia, Liberty University is a private, coeducational, undergraduate and graduate institution offering 55 undergraduate and 32 graduate programs serving over 11,300 residential students and 24,000 distance learning enrollment students. Individuals from all 50 states and more than 80 nations comprise the diverse student body. While the faculty and students vary greatly, the common denominator and driving force of Liberty University since its conception is love for Jesus Christ and the desire to make Him known to the entire world.

For more information about Liberty University, contact:

Liberty University
1971 University Boulevard
Lynchburg, VA 24502
Telephone: 434-582-2000
www.Liberty.edu

Additional copies of this book and other book titles from DESTINY IMAGE are available at your local bookstore.

Call toll-free: 1-800-722-6774.

Send a request for a catalog to:

Destiny Image® Publishers, Inc.
P.O. Box 310
Shippensburg, PA 17257-0310

"Speaking to the Purposes of God for This Generation and for the Generations to Come."

For a complete list of our titles, visit us at www.destinyimage.com.